STEPPING
UP

STEPPING
UP

*The Art of Achieving Leadership
Excellence for Elevated
Team Performance*

AMAL ELTAHIR

JONES MEDIA
PUBLISHING

Stepping Up: *The Art of Achieving Leadership Excellence for Elevated Team Performance*

Jones Media Publishing
10645 N. Tatum Blvd. Ste. 200-166
Phoenix, AZ 85028
JonesMediaPublishing.com

Disclaimer:

The author strives to be as accurate and complete as possible in the creation of this book, notwithstanding the fact that the author does not warrant or represent at any time that the contents within are accurate due to the rapidly changing nature of the Internet. While all attempts have been made to verify information provided in this publication, the Author and the Publisher assume no responsibility and are not liable for errors, omissions, or contrary interpretation of the subject matter herein. The Author and Publisher hereby disclaim any liability, loss or damage incurred as a result of the application and utilization, whether directly or indirectly, of any information, suggestion, advice, or procedure in this book. Any perceived slights of specific persons, peoples, or organizations are unintentional.

In practical advice books, like anything else in life, there are no guarantees of income made. Readers are cautioned to rely on their own judgment about their individual circumstances to act accordingly. Readers are responsible for their own actions, choices, and results. This book is not intended for use as a source of legal, business, accounting or financial advice. All readers are advised to seek the services of competent professionals in legal, business, accounting, and finance field.

Printed in the United States of America

ISBN: 978-1-948382-89-2 paperback

To my husband and kids, whose constant inspiration fuels my endeavors.

To my extended family, team, and best friends, for invaluable support throughout my growth journey.

And a tribute to anyone who has ever dared to step up and make a difference. This is for you, the dreamers, the doers, the ones who believe in the power of positive change.

TABLE OF CONTENTS

THE CITY MANAGER

First and foremost: "It takes two to tango"

— Al Hoffman and
Dick Manning

The role of a city manager extends beyond that of a typical executive. It encompasses a more parental and nurturing responsibility. City managers play a vital role in the effective functioning of city organizations. They bring in leadership value and business management expertise to ensure that city organizations are well-structured and capable of providing essential services that meet the needs of their communities. It is important to recognize that cities, like individuals, possess distinct characteristics and personalities and may undergo a range of experiences. They encounter both favorable and challenging times. They can go through moments of triumph, failure, pain, growth, and decline. So, they can rise and can very much collapse. Ultimately, communities are responsible for shaping their own destinies and achieving their aspirations. As such, they can support or impede their own growth and development. Similar to a parent or a shepherd, the city manager strives to facilitate that growth process, yet the ultimate outcome—success or failure—rests in the hands of the community itself.

Regardless of the form of government, City managers and administrators help their elected officials and communities with focus, visioning, steering the course of the ship, and orchestrating both the planning and execution processes to achieve community objectives. They operate within the context of a regulatory environment and an emotional connection with the community they serve. They guide their team, orchestrate efforts, coordinate communications, and shoulder the responsibility of managing the community's business and its current and future health, but they also develop an emotional bond with their cities. They are chief advisors and top advocates for their community's wellbeing. They collect, digest, and reflect on enormous amounts of information to advise their elected officials to make informed decisions and help them understand the short and long impact of those decisions. They are the watchdogs protecting community interests. They become champions of the city's aspirations and stewards of its future. The city manager, the shepherd, fiercely defends and battles, both within and beyond, for the health, safety, and well-being of the community. A cheerleader and a coach for their team, the city manager, like a responsible parent, works tirelessly to create an environment that enables their team to thrive, adapt, and overcome obstacles.

Public Policy Context

What distinguishes a city from any other form of organization is this complicated relationship with the public, the diversity of issues and forces at play, and the magnitude and nature of impacts. We, as public administrators, organize this giant mostly through policy and planning processes. Scott Campbell and Susan Fainstein defined planning as the "intervention with the intention to alter the existing course of events." Why? Because the alternative is chaos and a destructive manifestation of self-interest and selfishness. This gets us into economics and the social impact of individual choices. My point is, based on current conditions, and using social science, we look into the future and predict outcomes. If the outcomes are not favorable, we plan to mitigate and work to fix it proactively. That is really the essence of and is why economic development, land use, housing, and nuisance control policies are founded. That is the reason why some cities seem to do better than others. Some are successful pleasant environments to be in and some are not.

When formulating plans, making decisions, and implementing policies, cities aim to address challenges, promote growth as a strategy for improving conditions, and improve public welfare. However, sometimes the impact of our public policies and decisions, or at least the perception of, can vary, suggesting differing outcomes for individuals, groups, or sectors. Policy decisions such as zoning and public infrastructure are concerned with collective benefit and public interest, often create winners and losers and can bring about substantial emotional impacts. But at the end of the day, they are for the benefit of the collective despite seeming otherwise for the individual. Those decisions are made for health, safety, and welfare. They are based on efficiency, equity, and market conditions and always for collective benefit. What does success look like?

A balance of idealism and Pragmatism

Success lies in striking a balance, maximizing benefits, minimizing costs, when tradeoffs are reasonable and when the people understand and accept the "why." Our communities accepted the democratic process where the majority rules. At the end of the day, we are on the same side. City managers are nonpartisan and impartial. We follow rational planning and a democratic process. We manage business to the best of our abilities and our end goal will always be serving the public interest. It is a balancing act and more art than science because we are in a people business. This complexity is what makes the job of a city manager both interesting and extremely challenging. The political environment we operate in often gives rise to fallacies and breeds conflict opportunists, whose objective is to manipulate narratives to exploit dissent, emotional outbursts, and public outcry. Success is momentum because what we do is a long game and success is in resilience and in making progress despite obstacles.

Policy decisions often involve complex issues and trade-offs. Therefore, achieving universal agreement on those decisions is mission impossible, as it is extremely difficult to please everyone with an outcome. Handling emotional outbursts and public outcry requires patience, empathy, courage, and effective communication. It is important for city managers to understand the importance of leading the narrative and consider the potential winners and losers when formulating and implementing policies. While the public interest is inherently collective, mitigating the negative consequences for disadvantaged groups and ensuring equitable distribution of benefits and cost burden contribute to more inclusive and sustainable policy outcomes. In a nutshell, the process makes all the difference. The process ought to include public participation and communication, stakeholder engagement, and evaluation of impacts to help identify and address any unintended or disproportionate effects on specific individuals or groups. Will everyone agree with policy decisions? Absolutely not. It is highly unlikely that everyone will agree with policy decisions all the time. People have different perspectives, values, interests, and priorities, which can lead to differing opinions on various policy matters. Different individuals may have diverse ideologies and priorities, which shape their stance on specific decisions. We are not always aligned in how we define values and priorities. The trick is getting people to step out of their perception and into perspective to understand and see the big picture. Even when we see the big picture, we don't always agree on how we get there. So, we have to subscribe to the idea of a team and proper organization systems.

Being a City Manager is not glamorous. City managers are preoccupied with the future and concerned mostly with the long game. They serve as chief executive officers to their organization, guiding their team to create and sustain success. But unlike any other executive director, they manage day-to-day business and end up dealing with issues and complaints eight to five. Issues escalated daily to the city manager. Not for lack of capable staff, but because of the nature of what we do. When staff are stuck, they involve the city manager because the stakes are high and can turn political very quickly. Inherently, regulation, property rights, entitlement, and code enforcement generate a lot of unhappy people and our development process such as street closures and traffic construction inconveniences them. For the residents to feel better, they would like to appeal their case to the City manager. This is rooted in the complicated relationship with the public and the conflicting expectations. The public are our customers who we provide services for, the stakeholders who are impacted by our decisions and represented by the direction we take, and the taxpayers who fund our operations, but they are also on the receiving end of our enforcement. Good customer service here has a different definition depending on the situation and the hat they are wearing. We should be ready to address anyway they show up. For example, they hold us accountable for the quality of our park's facilities and the opportunity for recreation in them, at the same time, they don't want to pay the additional taxes that support those expectations. We understand that the public are entitled to receive our attention. But, the capacity for addressing all concerns swiftly is limited. Therefore, we organize through processes and build a prioritization system. We have to respect the process to be orderly. We can not just drop everything to address what one individual might consider a priority or an emergency.

STAKEHOLDERS: POLICY REPRESENTING THEIR IDEAL	TAXPAYER: FUNDING OUR OPERATIONS FISCALLY RESPONSIBLE	RECEIVER OF SERVICES RESPONSIVE TO NEEDS & GENEROUS WITH OPPORTUNITY	RECEIVER OF COMPLIANCE & ENFORCEMENT FAIR TREATMENT

Customer Expectation Changes According to the Hat they are Wearing

Being a city manager is taxing. The hardest part of being there is dealing with the stress. No matter how good you are at what you do, unless you can deal with the stress of it, it burns you. This is why handling the role of the city manager is not merely about qualifications but more of a question of disposition. City managers do the work that no one else wants to do.They spend a great deal of time smoothing egos and confronting negative thoughts, to ensure a harmonious and positive environment. They make decisions that no one wants to make. They deal with the difficult people no one wants to deal with. They get called on to resign and are more likely to live a "constructive discharge" situation because of their advocacy, decisions or the direction they are taking that may not serve some individuals. Constructive discharge is defined as living in a hostile or intolerable work environment that is worthy of prompting resignation, according to the Department of Labor.

The diversity of issues dealt with is mind boggling. One day they are dealing with the naked guy at the park, a feral cat's mess, that guy who doesn't like their neighbor and wants the city to do their bidding for them. The next day they are dealing with the guy who is upset with the city for displaying "nativity scene" at the park, the guy who is picking a fight with the city because he is still bitter because of rightful code enforcement, and the lady who wants staff to drop everything they are working on to go take care of the tree branches that are bothering her and another for allowing a parade to happen. People not getting along will try to involve the city. Those who are holding a grudge against the city will not miss an opportunity to shoot themselves in the foot. Just for the record, the city cannot be part of a personal vendetta or prejudice in any shape or form. We will uphold our values and treat everyone the same. And no, we are not going to fire staff for doing their job, enforcing city code. Let us just say that they are of service to their staff and the public during the day tackling those "ankle biters" as Tyler Trout calls them. They are running a marathon and those "ankle biters" are slowing them down. Their real work actually starts at five in the evening, when everybody leaves because their responsibility is way beyond the trivial business and hand holding. City managers are not there to please individuals. They are there to protect and advance collective interests, operationalize an agreed upon community vision, and help their city navigate and avoid disruptive challenges.

City managers are architects of budgets and resource planning, in a constantly changing world. They operate within a highly regulated environment and a mandated process, to meet public expectations that can be quite demanding and, most of the time, unrealistic. I just gave you an example of those conflicting customer expectations. We find ourselves caught between market forces and public impacts, navigating state legislative impacts and reluctant Councils. Managers, especially in small cities, are challenged with figuring it all out with a skeleton crew, I repeat: skeleton crew, while dealing with small town politics, "ankle biters", and conspiracy theorists who have got all the time in the world to stir nonsense, spread ignorance, and waste public resources. Whether making it work by adopting robust approaches such as coming up with alternative funding sources and shared service models or resorting to priority-based budgeting that requires gladiators to push through the wall of "CAVE" and a small town politics combo, to make ends meet. CAVE is the term that has been used for decades to describe those citizens against virtually everything. How motivated are you? What kind of incentive is driving you to bear all of this nuisance? You have been riding a bull yourself, how are you going to keep your team engaged and motivated?

They are also concerned with addressing complex social issues. Their role expands with the role of their government. For example, COVID-19 pandemic redefined what good governance looks like. It changed community expectations. In addition to being participatory and transparent, governments now ought to be capable, agile, and innovative. You rely on your local government to intervene and to take the lead in tackling the problem, if needs are otherwise not being met. The dilemma is city managers must make sure the government's social role does not expand beyond its domains and fiscal capacity, while maintaining equity. Should you fully fund an animal shelter, knowing something else has to give? We are mostly property tax funded. But the property tax system is too limited to support the challenges we face. And user fees can have a serious impact on affordability and equal access to our programs and services, resulting in poor outcomes. You would like help but you know for sure that if you did some people would not afford their water bill.

Much like a new parent caring for a newborn, city managers cannot afford to take their eyes off the responsibilities before them. They are responsible for the people who are responsible for making sure everyone is safe. They get that call if one of their staff got injured in an altercation or a fire incident. They strive to propose value-adding policies and make organizational decisions that address current and future needs and aspirations of a broad range of stakeholders. However, the city council and community control the outcomes. "You can lead a horse to water, but you can't make it drink." And it is inevitable that some people will hold dissenting opinions, either due to differing beliefs or the perception that their interests are not adequately represented. Success here means striving for alignment and requires understanding and continuous learning and embracing the fact that "falling" and setbacks are just part of the process.

City Managers live and operate in a highly visible environment, where their moves and actions are under the microscope and constant public scrutiny. This visibility complicates both their social life and decision-making process, making them more susceptible to criticism and opposition. This is a huge disadvantage because some people don't know or don't care about the difference between personal and business. Things are not always as they appear to be. An incomplete picture is tricky. "Little knowledge is a dangerous thing"-Alexander Pope. Some resort to personal attacks if they don't have a valid business argument and can't find another way to aim at the city manager. Unfortunately, the impact extends to family members including innocent children. What compensates for that hazard?

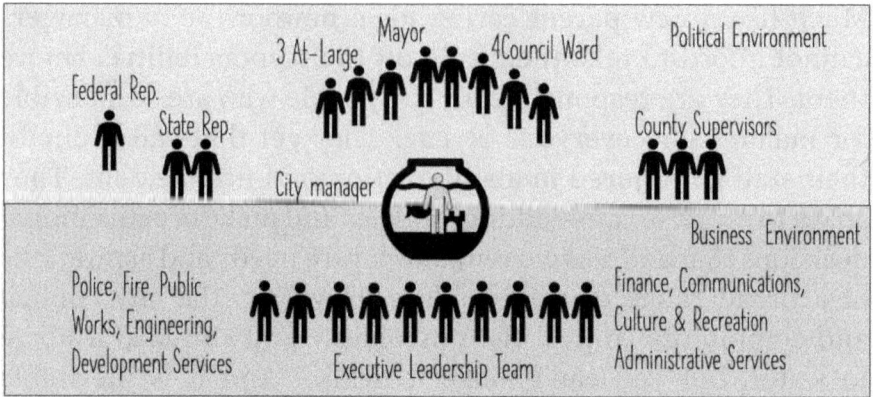

The City Manager's World. Living in a Fishbowl. The figure shows the city manager's span of control. The city manager serves as the bridge between the business environment and the political environment. Idea Credit: Patti Seda

"When you can't see someone all day long, the only thing you have to evaluate is the work." —Jason Fried

The city manager evaluation process is flawed due to incompatible expectations and scale. Does it make sense that city managers be responsible for the long-term yet are evaluated based on short-term or an annual criteria. Doesn't make sense and is highly subjective. Governments inherently operate on longer timelines, and it takes heaven and earth for them to move an inch. Achieving meaningful results often requires multiple years and a supportive community. That's why strategic plans are done in a three-to-five-year span. The discrepancy between the long-term nature of their role and the short-term evaluation period can create challenges in terms of accurately assessing their performance and the impact of their strategic decisions. I wouldn't call them evaluations. I do consider them check-in points to level-set rather than evaluations.

Why would anyone want to be a city manager? Despite the complexity of the city manager's role, the opportunity to participate in shaping communities' futures and positively impacting the daily lives of individuals is fulfilling. Knowing and seeing the difference between has and could have been is vastly stimulating. I have always been part of winning teams. Working with great people and solving complex problems are the things that make me tick. Connecting the dots is my superpower. I see the interconnectedness and understand the complexity of our world and the broader system in which we operate. Bad actors and difficult circumstances don't define me. I don't ever regret choosing this path and am passionate about my process. Finding joy in the company of others, my true satisfaction lies in how well the goals we pursue as a team align with my values. It's my drive and my reward.

The relationship between the city manager and their community is similar to marriage in that both parties, the city, and the manager, are intertwined and reflect on each other. The city manager serves the public interest, while the city reflects the manager's leadership. The city and I have embarked on a journey together. Here I am two years later, vested in this marriage. But I know, it will take two to tango. Commitment and understanding are what we need to nurture growth and development, both for me and for the city.

Take Away

City governments are intricate and rewarding entities to manage. Effective management revolves around achieving a delicate balance. Public policy making is the art of finding balance, navigating the process, and working towards the greater good. We strive to minimize costs and maximize benefits for the community. Success lies in following a transparent and rational decision-making process. Decisions require due diligence, gathering a substantial amount of information and making sense of it all, and communicating a comprehensive understanding of the factors at play.

The bond between a city manager and their city involves a deep sense of commitment, attachment, and understanding. It goes beyond the technical aspects of managing business. A city manager must connect with their community, embrace its aspirations, and work diligently to fulfill its collective vision. By understanding the unique qualities of their team and buying into the dreams of their communities, city managers can lead with passion, contributing to the overall well-being and success of their cities, tackling challenges and not letting limitations keep the team from achieving remarkable things. Constructive dialogue and accountability in the policy-making process can help foster understanding and minimize disagreement. It is essential to listen to different perspectives, take feedback into account, and communicate the rationale behind plans and decisions. While complete consensus may be elusive, striving for inclusivity can somewhat enhance the effectiveness of policy outcomes.

BEYOND BUSINESS:
"MUSIC IN THE SOIL"

"The greatness of a community is most accurately measured by the compassionate actions of its members."

– Coretta Scott King

Oskaloosa, Iowa, is a remarkable place. While it may be difficult to pinpoint the exact stimulus that elicits such a profound connection, there is undoubtedly something about it that touched the depths of my soul. Maybe the small- town charm and unique character that captures hearts. Or its undeniable resemblance to a city that occupies a special place in my heart, Iowa City. A city that flexes a rich history and an intimate environment that forwards a sense of security and places a real Iowa experience is heaven to any architecture junkie. This warm atmosphere cultivated a close-knit community where individuals are heavily involved.

The deep sense of connection and warmth experienced in Oskaloosa may stem from the quality relationships that thrive within its borders. The experience here is authentic and enriching. I had the opportunity to meet fascinating individuals who gave me insights into the livability of a place that offers ample opportunity for joyful living. A small city, big heart, complete, a melting pot, charming, and full of prospects and opportunity for personal growth. The pace is faster than what I was expecting. The scenes and interactions unfolding before you are intense like a captivating novel, carrying a touch of intrigue. A feeling that added depth to the overall experience, making it even more evocative. Tense, challenging, and occasionally overwhelming, nevertheless, overall, my experience is positive and worthwhile.

A "great place" often offers a combination of a range of factors that come together to create a unique experience. While the perception of a "great place" can vary from person to person, there are certain elements that tend to contribute to its appeal. Oskaloosa has a distinct character that sets it apart. Its identity is influenced by its long and rich history and local traditions. The urban core is also home to rural identity. You can almost touch the dividing line. The unique qualities and elements of celebration contribute to its authenticity and make it forever memorable.

People like stories and we tend not to forget how we felt. Psychologists say experience is an imprint of how we felt at the time and feeling of joy is merely a manifestation of reality or construct of reality. It's not like we can help it. It's how we are programmed. Our brains may register some or all details of an event creating a memory, but our subconscious is in a continuous mission of accumulating how we feel and attaching those feelings to pictures our brains register. Truth my friends, we do fall in love with places just like we do fall in love with people. One might not know how to describe or pinpoint the exact moment in time they fell in love with their loved ones. They just know and the accumulation of experience of joy and connection happens over time.

The visual appeal plays a significant role in creating those attachments to Oskaloosa. Masterpiece level architecture, and the attractively preserved facade and streetscape dare to evoke emotions, prompting admiration and attachment. No doubt, the grand band stand of 1912 by Frank E. Wetherell, the Book Vault, High Avenue, and the Lamberson and Alsop House by Frank

Lloyd Wright, the old post office, and the City Square Park are my most breathtaking landmarks. A friend of mine called it "a scene from a Hallmark movie." Nonetheless, for a city person, this calm beauty contributes to its allure. A prototype for Iowa. This city is the beating heart of Mahaska County. Generous and nondiscriminatory. Exploited and resented. Its countryside has a way of inspiring those who explore it. My friends are raving about natural habitats, pheasants, and the magnificent recreation trail around the city. I have to admit, while hunting and camping aren't really my thing, I do appreciate a hike or a bike ride on that trail.The peacefulness and serenity found in those surroundings provides solace and rejuvenation for the souls.

The people of Oskaloosa truly embody the essence of what makes the city special. Their warmth, humility, elegance, and genuine care is inspiring. They are very protective of their legacy. They take pride in their ability to make great things happen and have successfully preserved the city's greatness, which was once on the verge of slipping away. They are overprotective and may act like a helicopter mom . Their dedication to saving and improving their surroundings has left a profound mark and will undoubtedly leave a legacy. And of course, like any other community, there are those who can be a disgrace to the human race. The misguided, blind ignorant, self-serving, envious, and full of hate. Those are the outliers. They tend to be very loud and disruptive. But contrary to their belief, they don't represent the broader Oskaloosa community by any means.

Whether engaging in conversations with the caring natives or the invested implants, or witnessing incredible acts of kindness, observing the genuine connections and authentic interactions among the people of Oskaloosa is an experience that changes you forever.

Take Away

The allure of Oskaloosa is deeply personal and subjective. For me, it is a place where a sense of belonging takes root, and where love for the experience grows within. Everyone may have their own unique reasons for falling in love with Oskaloosa, but the collective essence of its charm, architecture, and people contribute to its undeniable appeal. Or maybe Mia Reed was right. She told me there is "music in the soil".

STEPPING UP

Welcome to "Stepping Up". This book is a modest attempt to share observations, thoughts, and the lessons learned. Drawn from personal experiences and a bit of trial and error, I humbly invite you to explore the art of leading with a growth mindset, embracing imperfections and uncertainties. Beyond the narrative lies a compass for understanding city dynamics and the significance of collective growth, all underpinned by a growth mindset.

Let's dive into the heart of leadership excellence using a city manager's goggles. The narrative includes strategies for unlocking the potential within your team and for creating a workplace where learning and development are celebrated, and improvement is not a destination but a continuous pursuit. In these pages, we explore the essence of growth and team mindset, justifying why and showing how it can revolutionize leadership in the modern workplace. From the fast-paced dynamics of city leadership to the intricate world of public service, we navigate through the challenges that leaders face. The goal? To equip you with insights and strategies to not only lead effectively but to inspire and elevate team's performance.

As we unfold the chapters, you'll discover a framework for organizational effectiveness that goes beyond the ordinary. Learn how aligned leadership and business strategy can create a ripple effect, positively impacting communities and fostering excellence. We explore an approach to public service leadership that transforms, adapts, and leaves a lasting impact. Ready to step up? Let's embark on this transformative journey together.

CHAPTER 1

A NEW BEGINNING

"The beginning is the most important part of the work."

— Plato.

As I stepped into the role of City Manager of Oskaloosa Iowa, I could not help but feel a mix of excitement and responsibility. What did I get myself into? The City's name was whispered with pride, and I was determined to make my mark. I like beginnings because they are filled with hope and positive energy. With a sense of anticipation, I set out to understand the inner workings of the community and its unique challenges. Ready for my learning journey.

My first undertaking was to immerse myself in the City's dynamics, history, position, and culture. I delved into conversations, pouring over history and aspirations, listening to the thoughts traversed caring minds. It was through these glimpses into the past and perspectives into the future that I began to understand the city's deep-rooted values and traditions. I believe understanding the past can indeed provide valuable insights and perspective when making decisions about the future. While I may not be bound by tradition, acknowledging history and the broader context of experience will help my journey in shaping direction and influencing choices moving forward.

I just left a community fully saturated with its essence and deeply attuned to its needs. A community where I was fully immersed in its culture and aware of its struggles. Now, I am embarking on a new chapter, venturing into uncharted territory. I am not referring to familiarity with public affairs or managing business. I am talking about the process of building a connection with a brand new personality of a community. My goal would be to bond with and find Oskaloosa's true north to help guide my city towards a brighter future and of course to enjoy what indeed pays my soul.

City organizations are tasked with various responsibilities and functions and are responsible for providing essential services such as planning for and maintaining infrastructure, managing public safety, regulating growth and land use, etc. They also play a vital role in promoting community development, fostering economic growth, and ensuring the well-being of residents. For a city manager, this includes working to address the apparent needs and concerns of the community and the problems they probably do not know they have. Therefore, success in the job requires a great deal of trust. Much like a doctor who conducts a thorough set of tests and comes up with a prognosis and a plan to prevent an imminent malfunction or to annihilate the cancer or to shield you from the infection you cannot see. Sometimes, you must have faith in their expertise and judgment. City managers focus on and study cities. They have the mental framework to help them make connections invisible to the average person and enable them to anticipate potential outcomes. We know all about cities. Not because we are all geniuses. No, because cities and city business are what we chose to focus on. You could, too, if you have the passion for it. Our expertise shapes how we perceive and interpret the world around us. That level of awareness is more of a curse than a blessing. Trust me, I couldn't not pay attention to what is going on, even if I wanted to.

The city itself is a delicate ecosystem, with each element interconnected and dependent on one another. It scares me sometimes looking at the fragility of its position. Just as in a thriving forest, where every organism plays a role, every institution has a part to play in shaping the community's destiny. Good or bad. Nothing is in a vacuum. My goal is to add value and run an organization, fostering collaboration and forging partnerships and connections. As the guardian of the big picture, it is also my duty to protect priorities, well-being, point out damaging actions, and expose misbehavior. The city manager, the hammer, has to sometimes be hard on the players. With this rich ecosystem and the body being in motion, it is my strategy to timely catalyze to amplify impacts and fire up my ripple effect. Make no mistake, I will contain infections and remove cancers, if I have to. We cannot jeopardize our mission. Not on my watch nor am I willing to fail or neglect my duty. I will not associate my name with a failing team ever.

To understand the town's inner workings, I dove into its history and engaged with people. I was captivated by the stories shared by the community's greatest fans and troubled by the stories that some conspiracy theorists genuinely believed. Talking about triumphs and struggles, each narrative revealed a layer of the community's identity, providing me with valuable insights into its past and the foundation on which it stood. The energy I sense from invested leadership is refreshing and assuring. Just as a puzzle comes together piece by piece, I gather my information, analyzing data, identifying the challenges that lie ahead, and examining the city's infrastructure, its local economy, and its social fabric. With each observation, I gained a clearer picture of the city's strengths and weaknesses, its opportunities, and threats.

For me challenges are not insurmountable obstacles but rather opportunities for growth and achievement. Getting through with discipline and a resilient mindset that learns from setbacks, seeks support, and celebrates milestones. I always believed it was possible to navigate the racecourse and emerge victorious in my pursuits. I quickly recognized that progress required thoughtful planning and bold action. As an architect designing a grand building, I sketched my plan for engaging the players to develop a unified vision for the future, picturing a place that would be both resilient and vibrant. Then together we build the blueprint that organizes and guides all our efforts. Oskaloosa is blessed with an unmatched wealth of community partners who care. But the challenge remained: how do we get there? This community's obsession with independence and autonomy created too many divisions. This might have worked well in the past, but given today's limiting circumstances and need for togetherness, I would say not going to work. We need to shift our mindset. Misunderstandings created a wedge between key players and of course change aversion is typically to blame for more delays.

Change can elicit various reactions and responses. Some individuals resist change, feeling uneasy or anxious about the unknown. Every time I think about change, I remember Mark Twain's quote just to manage my own expectations. For the chuckles, it is: "The only person who likes change is a baby with a wet diaper." Why? It disrupts comfort. We are wired to avoid discomfort. The familiarity of the status quo can feel safer and more predictable compared to the uncertainty that change brings. However, logically, it's important to recognize that change is inevitable and is necessary for growth and progress. While change can be uncomfortable or daunting, it is an inherent part of life. For a city manager, change and growing pains are part of the process. Because when it comes to community business, nothing is easy. Change is either a byproduct or an especially important measure to realize a goal. The trick is getting change-averse people to realize that change is inevitable and necessary for growth and development and sometimes necessary to maintain basic needs. In those instances where you are working on a long-term outcome, you need to elicit both patience and faith. All the roads to success lead back to the need for trust. I can't emphasize this enough. What should I do?

Conflict resolution became my priority to connect key stakeholders, bridging the gap between the different perspectives and uniting the players under shared purpose, despite the undeniable rural and urban tensions. Rural mindset might never trust those urban ambitions. Resentment has taken root. So, with the strategic planning process, I aimed to harmonize the voices of the community partners, validating and empowering them to actively participate in shaping the community's destiny. Seeing the tide of inbound state policy impact, this community has no choice but to join forces. Armors and blindfolds ought to come down. Leaders need to see what we are up against before it is too late. We are in the boat together and it has a hole. What are we going to do about it?

The trick is to see the big picture. Adversity has this remarkable ability to bring people together. In the face of challenges, individuals often find strength, resilience, and a shared purpose. Adversity unites us by transcending differences and encouraging collective action. When confronted with adversity, people realize that their common struggles outweigh their individual disparities. They recognize the universal human experience of facing obstacles and the need for mutual support. Adversity erases superficial divisions, such as status or background, as people come together to overcome shared hardships. I hope we see the need to stick together.

My role as City Manager is not just about solving immediate problems but it is about fostering long-term sustainability and building for the future. I always believed in growth. Like a farmer tending to their garden, I sought to nurture the city's potential, planting seeds, inviting innovation, and creating an environment where great ideas grow and blossom. My point is farmers are patient. With each passing day, my understanding of the city deepened, and my commitment grew stronger. Being a community steward is a privilege and a weight on my shoulders. I believe my actions would have a lasting impact, shaping the town for years to come. I am not planning on falling short. Architect Daniel Burnham once said: "Make no little plans, they have no magic to stir men's blood." The realization of the great Chicago plan required immense effort, dedication, and sacrifice. It was a result of hard work, discipline, and perseverance, accompanied by physical exertion and personal struggles. As a leader, I understood the weight of responsibility that came with my endeavor. For Oskaloosa's future, I am fighting fiercely, putting in every ounce of my determination. It is a battle, requiring me to give my all, fighting tooth and nail to overcome obstacles and to help make our vision a reality. I know the journey will be marked by sweat and even bloodshed, metaphorically speaking. Sacrifices are made in pursuit of greater visions. Double the dreadfulness when a community fights within. Fighting ignorance, selfishness, and backwardness. Goodness tends to favor abundance. Airports are generous. Their benefits spill over and have a ripple effect on local economies. Let's dive into this later.

Key Takeaway

Stepping into the role of City Manager was indeed a new beginning, filled with excitement and responsibility. As I embarked on this journey, I embraced the interconnectedness of the city's elements and the power of its history and recognized the potential for a brighter future. Guided by a sense of purpose and armed with determination, I set out to navigate the challenges, foster cooperation, and lead towards progress. Like a farmer looking to nurture, bring forth a new chapter in the city's story, one marked by unity, growth, and prosperity.

CHAPTER 2

WHAT PAYS YOUR SOUL?

"Never doubt that a small group of thoughtful, committed citizens can change the world; indeed, it's the only thing that ever has."

—Margaret Mead

I have always appreciated connecting with people and having a delightful intellectual conversation. My new role brought excitement and anticipation for meaningful relationships, understanding that they would also serve as the foundation for collaboration, progress, and my job joy. Each interaction I have with people is a thread, connecting me to the diverse tapestry making up the community. These relationships have the capacity to potentially enable us to work together in sync, propelling us towards our shared goals.

A city manager cannot operate in isolation. For the time I have been in the workforce, I have been observing social dynamics, paying special attention to how progress is made. I have learned from the masters that collaboration is essential for effective leadership and positive outcomes and that achieving success in community endeavors depends on establishing and nurturing good relationships. Therefore, and from the get-go, I have prioritized bridging gaps, connecting with my team, stakeholders, and partners, seeking to connect and learn more about their perspectives for a fully rounded one. Through countless coffee meetings and community conversations, I started to build my network of connections that would prove invaluable in years to come.

Recognizing the significance of the wedge between urban and rural, city and county, I was firm in my commitment to making progress. During my first week and at the tail end of a long court battle regarding a proposed regional airport plan, I walked into the county board of supervisors' office and introduced myself as their new partner. Wearing the "new guy" hat, I engaged in a bold dialogue about the airport focused on facts and actively listened to concerns. Beyond the noise of skepticism, I sought to bridge the gap. What ought to unite us is utterly significant and far beyond hard feelings and bruised egos. Matters at hand call for a reset. We are here today, and history is in the making. No doubt, true leadership requires audacity, envisioning the future, and taking decisive action. Controversy cannot deter a true leader from making the right move. Deep wounds. But, with grace we pull through the tough times. Courage is a prerequisite for effective leadership. We will rise from the ashes, but the burning comes first and success is in the work we are avoiding. My friends, the way out is always through. Always.

It quickly became apparent that the decision-making process and the communication between the two were in dire need of repair. Tied at the hips, we ought to work on why there is a dissent. However, being transparent about our vision and intentions, we witnessed the transformative power it holds. Building relationships and mending broken bridges is possible when we try to connect and communicate honestly and openly. At the end of the day, we are in the same boat. It's a long game, but by approaching the board with respect and desire for a positive change, we paved the way for progress. This genuine exchange laid the foundation not only for amending relationships but working together towards a common goal. Only together can we address the challenges at hand and proceed with purpose.

In my conversations with local business owners and developers, I got a good sense of the heartbeat of the city's economy. They were the entrepreneurs and visionaries, the risk-takers who invested their time, energy, and resources into building thriving enterprises. Their perspectives are invaluable, like compasses guiding economic development and job creation, all pointing to our housing and infrastructure limitations. Through these connections, I gained a deeper understanding of their challenges and aspirations. I listened to stories of perseverance, dreams of growth, and concerns about regulations, infrastructure, and our future. Each conversation was like a window into their world, allowing me to comprehend the intricate dance between business and community, and helping in figuring out how to catalyze solutions that would benefit both. That is why we exist as an organization, to serve and add value to our community. The people and the businesses. I don't know how the communities and legislators lose sight of this fact.

Engaging with community leaders is equally crucial. They represent the pillars of the community, the individuals who dedicated their time, money, and expertise to serving the community's needs. Through regular touchpoints we create and maintain alignment. Together we advance the vision. Organizations such as "Mahaska County Community Foundation", "Rotary Club", "Optimist Club", "Lions Club" and the incredible "Golden Goose Club" organically formed and self-funded nevertheless have a profound impact on the livability of the community. I admit. I have never seen a model like "Golden Goose Club" anywhere.

So impactful and so considerate. With deep care and kindness, they supported collective efforts towards community objectives and significantly contributed to livability. I can only build on and contribute to aligning resources to leverage and augment their impacts.

We humans are social beings. We default to group. We define ourselves with groups. Whether that's your family, sports team, community, political party, association, or the college you went to. We'll strive to relate to a group and names unify us. It just must be a group of individuals sharing something of value. And we're also very unconsciously sentimental. We are drawn to stories. We orient ourselves in those stories and a lot of times see ourselves in them. We tend to want to relate.

During my first 100 days, I sat down with the mayor, city council members, City Staff, federal and state representatives, and representatives from various community organizations such as Oskaloosa School District, William Penn University, Indian Hills Community College, Mahaska Health, Main Street, Chambers, Mahaska County Conservation, Mahaska Rural Water, MidAmerican Energy, United Way, YMCA, etc. As well as connecting with neighboring and peer communities' leadership. Each encounter was an opportunity to align our visions, identify areas of collaboration, and address the pressing issues facing the community. Together, we form a network of support, a tapestry of leaders committed to the community's betterment.

Connecting with current and past state representatives is especially important as the state policy has a significant impact on community business, and its influence is closely interconnected with that of our local government. The average person often doesn't discern the distinction between impacts of these two levels of governance in their daily lives, complicating things for the city manager. Representatives, serving as lawmakers and advocates, play a vital role in representing community interests through input into program fundings and shaping the community's well-being through state legislation. It is crucial for cities to establish relationships and alignment with their representatives, ensuring alignment of efforts to avoid chaos that may arise from conflicting priorities and narratives. The city can serve as the data point for the representative as it is in touch with the needs of the community and has the means for scientific conclusions. In absence of that connection, there is a wide room for politics, anecdotal evidence, alternative truths, and subjectivity because we all know that the squeaky wheel gets the grease and the general public's memory is a very short one, equivalent to that of a goldfish and can be easily distracted.

Listening to concerned residents, especially those who lived or worked in Oskaloosa for a long time was at the heart of my learning journey and relationship-building efforts. They are the custodians of the city, the ones who lived and breathed its essence every day. Their insights are invaluable, reflecting the joys, concerns, and aspirations of the community at large. During my learning quest, I picked a handful of people to have a deep conversation with regarding sustainability and economic development. I had the opportunity to have a very enriching chat with a lifelong resident, a local farmer, and an investor who just picked Oskaloosa as a place to fulfill his vision and purpose. We talked about history, change, growth, today, and tomorrow. Those were my absolute delights that reinforced and renewed my commitment to this great community. Those conversations sharpened my perspective and enriched my soul.

And I very much enjoyed my conversations with Pat Sodak. This humble and intelligent individual injects positivity into the air, uplifting those around him. I appreciate the warm greetings from

City Hall and the patrons of City Square. I have learned a great deal and feel enriched in spirit. This is an example of community wealth and hidden gems and proof that the opportunity for giving and contributing is everywhere. You can simply contribute a great deal to your community by being positive and being a decent human being. Those small impactful moments are very assuring, enriching, encouraging, and uplifting. This part of my job pays my soul! Getting to know great people. Getting to enjoy delightful moments to undo the inevitable micro-disappointment encounters.

Through meetings and planning processes, I embarked on providing a platform for partners to voice their thoughts and concerns. Each conversation was an opportunity to bridge the gap between the city administration and the people, fostering both a sense of ownership and empowerment. Those perspectives and voices had an impact on and contributed to my understanding of community needs. Without a unified vision we are house-divided, chaotic, and fragmented. The community can support or impede its own growth. Remember, it takes two to tango. The community is responsible for its destiny and for shaping its future. My plan was to employ the strategic planning process as the first step in the budget process to make sure strategy and resources are aligned. As these relationships deepen, a sense of trust and mutual respect begins to blossom. Like the roots of a tree reaching deep into the soil, these connections form the bedrock of a small, united community. With this intentional communication process, the power of collaboration became evident as stakeholders from diverse backgrounds and interests confirmed common ground, working together towards our shared vision. The trick is to figure out how we synchronize together. Once again communication has proven to be a key and top priority that we will continue to work on.

In nurturing these relationships, I also emphasized the importance of reciprocity. I wanted to provide value and support to those I engage with. Whether it be connecting with resources, supporting initiatives, rooting for success, or advocating for concerns, I sought to be a catalyst for positive change, strengthening the bonds that held us together. Building relationships is not just a means to an end but a continuous process of growth and development. It requires active listening, care, and a genuine desire to understand and address the needs of others. I appreciate the perspectives, recognizing that they would shape the city's future trajectory. Having a shared vision for the future and a collective understanding of what we consider important can help us navigate challenges and conflicts more effectively. It provides a framework for decision-making and can build trust and strengthen our ability to communicate and collaborate.

Key Takeaway

To help the community realize its goals, it is essential to reach out to partners outside of City Hall and rebuild "burned bridges". Rebuilding takes time, effort, and a sincere commitment to open communication and collaboration. Collaboration could be in the form of embracing the discomfort of working with opposing viewpoints. Through active listening, reciprocity, and a commitment to understanding the diverse perspectives of the community, we catalyze and nurture unity. The strength of these relationships would determine the success of our collective efforts to shape a better future for the city.

Rebuilding Approach

Recognize strained or broken relationships that may have occurred in the past. Understand the reasons behind these fractures and acknowledge the impact they may have had on collaboration and progress within the community. Identify common goals and areas of collaboration between City Hall and external partners. This assessment helps with rebuilding relationships and working together towards shared objectives.

Plant the seed to encourage a culture of collaboration within the leadership team and the community. Promote open dialogue, inclusivity, and the sharing of resources and expertise. Initiate open and honest communication channels with those external partners. Reach out to express a genuine desire to rebuild relationships, and listen to their concerns and perspectives. Building trust and understanding through dialogue is crucial for rebuilding burned bridges. Identify and support opportunities for joint projects and initiatives. Engage all partners in discussions about these projects, seeking input and involvement early on. This approach fosters a sense of ownership and shared responsibility. Help define the roles of each partner involved. Clarity helps ensure that everyone understands their responsibilities and can work towards common goals effectively. Celebrate successes and those achievements resulting from collaborative efforts. Acknowledge the contributions of external partners and highlight the positive impact these partnerships have had on the community. The recognition encourages continued collaboration and strengthens relationships.

CHAPTER 3

WHAT IS LEADERSHIP?

"Leadership is a choice, not a rank."

—Simon Sinek

There is no such thing as organizational success without an engaged productive team. It does not exist. To create success that is going to outlast my tenure, I am investing in building a leadership team and a robust system for execution. My leadership strategy goes hand in hand with my business strategy but is arguably more important. Without a robust leadership strategy, visions end up sitting on shelves. My overarching goal is to build the most capable and effective team of teams to carry out the city's exceptional vision and to build a system that helps the team perform even when we are not at our best. Then, together, we have a significant positive impact. Almost all organizations have great visions but only those who figure out their alignment will make it.

What's leadership?

Let's step back and define leadership. I was sitting one day talking to my teenage son, Ahmad, and I asked him this question. Hey, what do you think leadership is? It didn't take him a second and

Leadership Strategy=

Approach, Values, & behavior (culture)

Business Strategy =

Strategic Business plan

Success is Aligning Leadership Strategy and Business Strategy

he replied: "Leadership is when you bring out the best in a group and help them work in harmony." He couldn't be more right and I couldn't be more proud of him. It hit me realizing that maybe it's the best definition of leadership I ever heard.

Over the years, my opinion has evolved to see leadership as conduct and a matter of choice, having both the capacity and mindset to connect with people and positively influence behavior. If you think about it, everything about it revolves around engaging with and representing people's ideals. Everyone is a potential leader and the opportunity to lead is all around us. You choose to take on the lead or not. You choose to embody ideal behaviors or whether to genuinely invest in people or not. That choice is reflected in how you conduct and express yourself. But to be called a leader, that version of you must be inspiring and worth emulating or listening to. It should represent the ideal values. It is also about having a vision and convincing people to follow that vision. Your leadership becomes evident through your ability to inspire, influence, persuade, and guide people. Contrary to the widespread belief, as a leader, you do not have to know everything. But you must be willing to act and have confidence in your capacity to address issues and know how to figure out who knows and let them help. Therefore, leadership is rooted in and tied to feelings such as confidence, courage, and trust that have to exist for people in order to follow you.

Courage: is the ability to act despite fear. It is the capacity for taking risks and is the willingness to step outside one's comfort zone, tackle those obstacles, and stand up for your principles or values, even in the face of risk and discomfort.

Confidence: is the opposite of doubt and what you project to people around you. It is a state of assurance born from a belief in your abilities and is reflected in your actions, decisions, and interactions with others.

Trust: is firm belief in your reliability, integrity, honesty, delivery, and judgment. It also involves a sense of assurance and a belief that the trusted party will act in good faith and fulfill those expectations.

Leadership is often confused with management. It is certainly not management. You lead people and manage tasks. Because it's about people, it is an art rather than a one-size-fits-all science. Conducting yourself as a leader entails stepping up to take responsibility and having the capacity to employ a unique blend of skills, qualities, and approaches that can vary, depending on the context and the individuals being led.

Leadership is parenting. It is about taking care of those around you. It is never about knowing the answer. It is about figuring out where the answer lies and cultivating solutions. We follow when we connect at some level with the leader and trust their capability to deliver. We trust their judgment and have confidence in their integrity. Therefore, competency is key. It can be that they speak our truth, they represent something we aspire to that we secretly want to be like them, or we believe they represent and can protect our interest. We take comfort in believing that they know what they are doing, they are correct, and they will take care of us.

Willingly following someone is a vote of confidence and evidence of trust. Therefore, developing leadership means developing character and requires growing capacity for building trust, adaptability, and understanding of the unique dynamics of each situation. What works in one context may not work in another. Effective leadership then is knowing when and how to appropriately apply a palette of leadership approaches or qualities ranging from visionary and transformational to servant and situational, to guide your team toward success.

The true value of leadership shines through when circumstances are tough, unclear, and chaotic. Therefore, it also requires foresight, competency, courage, grit, and resilience to bounce back and help the team do the same. It is in these moments that the impact of leadership is most evident. Often unnoticed is the work transpiring in the background. I have noticed that excellence happens mostly because of those unseen unrecognized leadership moments, everywhere in the organization. Yes, when people step up and do a marvelous job influencing the team around them, positively impacting outcomes. That's why I seriously believe success is collective effort. Hard to quantify but is equally valuable when leaders skillfully prevent disasters and sustain stability. When you see success. It is a team one.

Leadership in Public Service

Having experienced both realms, I've realized that leading an organization in public service is more demanding than leading a private sector one. This is largely because of differences in focus, responsibilities, and accountability structures. Public sector leaders face greater constraints in terms of flexibility in decision-making and team structure. This is because government processes are dictated and systems are generally traditional, risk averse, and prone to adversarial propaganda, therefore lacking propensity for innovation and far from being efficient. Excellence in leadership here requires a unique set of skills and qualities, top of which is courage, being bold enough to take calculated risks and live with the consequences, the ability to balance competing considerations, and navigating political landscapes, while maintaining public trust. The "fishbowl" effect (Seda), where every move is closely observed and analyzed, adds an extra layer of complexity, making effective leadership particularly challenging. Leaders in this environment are often vilified and misunderstood. They must prioritize transparency and should continually demonstrate integrity, resilience, and a commitment to public service values. Navigating those complex regulatory and political environments requires courage, skillful communication, and diplomacy. The public stage exposes processes to scrutiny, politics, and conspiracy theory lines of thought, making disruptive opposition more likely and long-range policy especially challenging. It is ridiculously easy to take things out of context and generate a counter narrative. This heightened visibility complicates both the decision-making and implementation processes and demands a high level of adaptability and perseverance.

Leadership is more art than science. While both sectors require strong qualities such as strategic vision, communication skills, and team building capacity, the context and priorities differ. In the private sector, organizations are typically evaluated based on their ability to effectively produce goods and services or achieve measurable goals with a primary focus on profitability. Leaders there navigate a competitive marketplace, making decisions to optimize financial outcomes. On the other hand, public sector leadership is centered around serving the public interest, often encompassing a broader set of objectives beyond financial gains where leaders navigate complex social, political, and community dynamics, striving to balance diverse interests for the greater good.

Key distinctions in leadership emphasis between the public and private sectors include how success is defined. Success in the public sector is assessed based on the impact on the public and the fulfillment of societal needs. Bear in mind that this is a moving target. That's why I really believe in targeting momentum (trend) rather than snapshot success, as along the journey there will always be mountaintops and valleys. Leaders here emphasize accountability, transparency, and effective governance to meet the needs of the public. So, focus here gives priority to the process over outcome. Ultimately, the success of the private sector is often gauged by financial metrics, while the success of public sector organizations is judged by their ability to meet the needs and interests of the public they serve, which is highly subjective. Our goal is to make people's lives better, but it is not always easy to define what that looks like. I was a private sector leader for over half of my work life. I built and managed countless sales, construction, and design teams with an eye on the bottom line. Here I am 100% in the people business and my target is moving. Our emphasis defines and dictates what success and growth look like for my organization and my team.

CHAPTER 4

UNLEASHING MAGIC

"No one can whistle a symphony. It takes a whole orchestra to play it."

— H. E. Luccock

Keep in mind, organizations are inherently team based. To be successful in any type of organization, besides having robust business management systems, we must have skillful leadership to guide the team towards successful delivery of the organizational mission. What high quality leadership does is ensure collective and constructive collaboration and maximize value to yield results that are remarkable and far greater than the sum of those individual efforts.

Great leaders have the ability to catalyze magic and infuse joy into the daily work life of their teams. Their leadership goes beyond tasks and responsibilities, creating an environment where personal growth, enthusiasm, positivity, and a sense of purpose flourish. They are warm and highly competent. Those people are impactful and admirable. Through inspiration and guidance, these leaders create a workplace atmosphere that is not only productive but also enjoyable and fulfilling for the individuals within their team. Organizations blessed with such leaders produce the most qualified talented individuals and leaders, and they maximize their potential productivity.

Why Invest in leadership? Investing in leadership is crucial because the quality of leadership directly impacts organizational productivity. The era of mere command and control management has evolved, and we now recognize the immense value that effective leadership brings to the forefront. Strong leadership is instrumental in fostering innovation and driving success. The private sector recognized the return on investment a while back, but the public sector is just catching up, as always.

The most successful organizations have succeeded because of their strong leadership strategy and team. More than ever, we need effective leadership to organize ourselves to conduct our business in a way that maximizes our chances of success, allowing us to excel and to be efficient, innovative, and productive. Skillful leaders aligned to a clear strategy are invaluable to organizations because their influence has a compounding effect on team impact. Their ability to guide, inspire, and make strategic decisions contribute to the team's success and have a ripple effect, amplifying the overall positive outcomes and achievements of the entire organization.

How? Effective leaders' model ideal successful behavior for their teams. They reframe and push for the impossible. They operationalize goals, objectives, and values. They figure out how to prioritize goals and help the implementation process simply by aligning personal and organizational valued goals. Why? because true motivation comes from within, and we cultivate joy in every step we take closer to our valued goal. They help the team with building a system that keeps commitment at 100% by focusing on the right priorities and the meaning behind what the team does and making sure that it aligns with who the team wants to be. That system with built in habits helps maintain effort during both best and worst times and staying on track when the team is not at their best. They share thoughtful and insightful points of view inviting outside the box thinking, they seek and provide opportunities for learning and growth, and most importantly they dare to step up and take risk and initiative.

From an organizational perspective, collaboration achieved through teamwork amplifies the impact of leadership, making it an indispensable aspect of organizational success. As part of a leadership strategy, it is imperative for public sector leaders to prioritize the development of a more robust leadership team and the cultivation of a collaborative fun, team-oriented environment. Then through communication and management systems align the leadership strategy with the business strategy for higher productivity. Sustaining productivity requires discipline, consistency, and commitment. Discipline ensures a structured and focused approach to work, while commitment fuels the perseverance needed to overcome challenges and see projects through to completion. Sticking to routine builds habits and ensures results. Without these essential elements, achieving sustained productivity becomes a considerable challenge. When discipline and commitment are ingrained in the work culture, productivity becomes a natural outcome, contributing to success and accomplishment. That is how productive high performing cultures are formed.

Growth

> *"The best time to plant a tree is 20 years ago, the second best is now"*
>
> —Chinese proverb

No doubt some people are natural leaders, but effective leadership is developable and high performing team leadership is trainable. We may be inexperienced, but all are capable and have the potential for being at that level of effectiveness through strategies that can help bring out the best version of individuals and teams.

According to the US Marine, "the most important criteria for being a leader is wanting to be one." (Sinek) The growth process starts with intention and full awareness of your personality traits, triggers, and needs and most importantly your impact on the people around you. Then make sure you orient yourself relative to the leadership competencies and the balance of your traits. Adopt a growth mindset and be intentional about building trust and learn how to build and maintain good relationships and how to communicate effectively to maintain team alignment with values, goals, and objectives. You have got to reach a point where you and your team are rowing in the same direction. Ground the team with the values that orient them. If you are not already there, it'll take learning and adjustment along the way before you get comfortable with your structure. Have the mindset for it. You must remember however, that growth is painful. Do your magic and cultivate the grit for it.

Improvement in leadership and team performance is a function of a couple of factors. Creating and sustaining the success of your team will depend on strategies for alignment, commitment to building character, and the level of your effectiveness. If you have momentum, don't mind the ups and downs. There will be disruptions. Sometimes, you may lose battles before winning the war. Learn when to concede but stay committed to your growth path and that of your team. The difference will become apparent over time.

As part of my strategy, I embarked on a mission to build, inspire, empower, grow, enable, and unite my team around the profound "why" that brings us together and our need for fulfillment and belonging. I am actively working on team engagement eliminating barriers and minimizing potential for misunderstandings by encouraging effective communication and kindness, and normalizing maintaining constructive dialogue. We are all seeking fulfillment in the work we do. Success happens when people are fully engaged, motivated, and feel they are respected and gaining by being part of the team. They could be respected and gaining and not knowing that fact. I say feel because people's reality is their perception.

In the public sector, the environment we operate in is demanding. It is a true leadership test. You can imagine the emotional problems that come with that. People who can't handle the pressure will struggle. Leaders must learn how to cultivate grit to endure and assist the team in navigating negativity and their own negative thoughts. The goal I set for myself is to be the leader I wish I had and to forge a tighter knit, more resilient family in the team, one armed with the skills to help each other grow and reach unparalleled heights.

"Happy employees ensure happy customers. And happy customers ensure happy shareholders—in that order." (Sinek Start with Why) We are a service organization. The people are the assets. So, my organization's productivity will grow through the growth of my team. As a leader who is in touch with who they are, they are my ultimate product and the very essence of my commitment. It is the journey itself that will bind and help guide us toward victory. And I am in love with the process.

To be an effective leader one ought to adapt and respond to the unique demands and expectations of the environment one is in. Leaders take the lead to set the tone and prioritize the wellbeing of people before themselves. Regardless of titles and formalities, our relationships in the workplace boil down to simple human relations and interactions. Whatever setting we are in, whether personal or professional, our fundamental needs remain the same. We all require respect and reciprocity to foster healthy and effective connections with others. Your answer is genuine care and treating others the way you want to be treated. It is that simple.

Level of Engagement Dictates Performance

Organizational performance is simply the performance of its people. Individuals play a fundamental role in the overall success and effectiveness of the organization. Elevating team performance depends on understanding the human element and on figuring out how to foster full engagement and commitment. High performing organizations excel in the ability to connect with and effectively lead their people. Their success lies in fostering strong connections, promoting effective communication, and implementing robust management and leadership practices that collectively contribute to superior team performance. Simply put, as a leader if you don't understand people, you can't run the business.

It is hard to accept but emotions do drive decisions and stories and narratives hold more power than statistics. Understanding the human element is fundamental to understanding the dynamics of business. Organizations striving for high performance must learn how to adapt to evolving expectations and the emotional needs to remain productive and competitive. A study conducted by McKinsey & Company highlights the changing dynamics in the workforce and the importance of understanding the diverse needs of employees. McKensey surveyed 15,366 workers in seven countries including the United States from November 2022 to January 2023 about job satisfaction, commitment, well-being, and self-reported performance.

According to the study employees fall into six categories: 11% quitters, 10% disruptors, 32% mildly disengaged, 38% reliable and committed, 5% double-dippers, and only 4% thriving stars. Basically, over a half can be considered somewhat disengaged. Top cited factors contributing to disengagement are inadequate compensation and lacking meaning and purpose. Governments are hard pressed to compete when it comes to compensation but the lack of meaning and purpose is worth looking into.

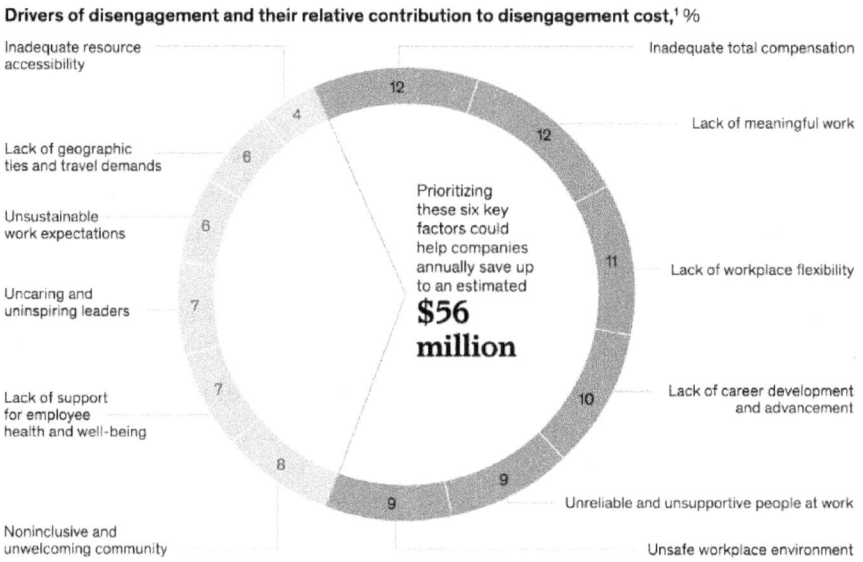

Drivers of disengagement and their relative contribution to disengagement cost,[1] %

Inadequate resource accessibility

Inadequate total compensation

12

12

Lack of meaningful work

4

Lack of geographic ties and travel demands

6

Unsustainable work expectations

6

Prioritizing these six key factors could help companies annually save up to an estimated

$56 million

11

Lack of workplace flexibility

Uncaring and uninspiring leaders

7

Lack of support for employee health and well-being

7

10

Lack of career development and advancement

8

9

Noninclusive and unwelcoming community

9

Unreliable and unsupportive people at work

Unsafe workplace environment

Drivers of Disengagement

Engagement Strategy

Leaders play a pivotal role in shaping the work environment and fostering employee well-being and fulfillment and therefore are critical for both engagement and productivity. They should put well-being and fulfillment at the forefront of their organizational priorities, as the performance of an organization depends on the performance of its people. Effective leaders understand that supporting and empowering individuals ultimately drive the success and longevity of the organization as a whole. The McKensey study breakdown of employees into six distinct groups underscores the need for tailored strategies to enhance satisfaction and productivity. It is not surprising at all that meaning and purpose came as a top factor influencing employee satisfaction. Leaders need to understand the diverse needs of their employees and the factors contributing to dissatisfaction to figure out an effective intervention strategy. They can also help with aligning individual values with organizational goals to enhance engagement. Your tools here are communication skills.

Clear and reinforced goals and objectives and being intentional about other subtle environmental cues can influence behavior. We tend to pursue our goals even when we are not consciously thinking about them, if we bought into them. The key is to understand, buy-in, and be able to describe those goals. Employees need to have a clear line of sight of those goals and values. They need to understand how they relate to what they do and what they can gain. That is all we need to emphasize clarity, and create the drive to perform. We don't need external incentives to pursue the goals that we value and believe in. Be intentional about this level of engagement.

Leaders should actively champion the well-being of their team members and should proactively address engagement issues by tailoring strategies to the specific needs of employees and the challenges associated with each employee's persona. By prioritizing satisfaction, leaders contribute to higher levels of engagement and by default retention within the organization. Keep in mind that people appreciate a supportive team that is fun and an honor to work with. I am not funny myself, but

I greatly appreciate humor because it lightens even the darkest moments. It lifts spirits and strengthens bonds among team members. Appreciating and encouraging humor can go a long way in creating a positive atmosphere.

Recommended Strategy Based on McKinsey's Employee Groups[1]:

Quitters (11%): Employees on their way out or already gone.

Strategy should focus on understanding reasons for departure and implementing long term retention measures.

Disruptors (10%): Actively disengaged individuals who can demoralize others.

Strategy: *Identify sources of dissatisfaction and provide constructive feedback and engagement to contribute to solutions or path forward. Understanding personalities and role expectations provides insights into dissatisfaction and assists with positioning. It is important not to hesitate in making tough decisions, including separating individuals who consistently contribute to a negative work environment. Clear communication and transparent processes are key in fostering a positive workplace and ensuring the overall well-being and productivity of the team.*

Mildly Disengaged (32%): Employees performing at the minimum level.

Strategy: Figure out what makes them tick. Regular check-ins and offering opportunities for skill development, particularly

---

[1] https://www.mckinsey.com/capabilities/people-and-organizational-performance/our-insights/some-employees-are-destroying-value-others-are-building-it-do-you-know-the-difference#/

in areas of interest, can significantly enhance employee engagement. It's important to figure out what motivates and interests everyone, understanding what makes them "tick." This approach not only contributes to professional growth but also strengthens the connection between employees and their work, fostering a more motivated and engaged team.

Reliable and Committed (38%): Employees consistently going above and beyond. *Strategy: Recognizing and rewarding dedication and providing growth opportunities are key. Be careful with spotlights as those are your typical subtle and modest personalities.*

Double-Dippers (5%): Individuals with multiple jobs.

Strategy: Address workload concerns and ensure transparency in policies. Visit with them to make sure you know what matters to them.

Thriving Stars (4%): Top talent bringing-in disproportionate value.

Strategy: *Recognition, challenging projects, and mentorship are essential to retain and motivate them.*

Key Points on Retention

The level of engagement and satisfaction among employees significantly influences their productivity, creativity, and dedication to organizational success and the collaboration and synergy among team members are critical factors in achieving organizational goals. Organizations often hire for competency, but it is the interpersonal skills and behavior that play a crucial role in employee retention. High performers are typically celebrated and maintained at all costs. However, those with demanding personalities, high drama or big egos, can introduce workplace conflicts. Coaching such individuals is challenging, especially when they view peers as rivals rather than collaborators. The competitive mindset impedes collaboration and undermines the leader's efforts to create a harmonious work environment, escalating conflicts within the workplace and leading to key team players leaving the team.

Organizational culture and values shape the behaviors and performance of individuals within the workplace. The saying "ego is the enemy" holds true in a team context. Individuals who believe they are superior to others can negatively impact the team and become a drain on organizational resources. Their detrimental influence often outweighs their super contributions.

Investing in the development of individual talents and skills contributes to the enhancement of organizational capabilities. However, be careful who you are giving a platform to speak, as promoting individuals with the wrong personalities and values can have adverse effects on workplace culture. Not addressing concerns is detrimental to the team spirit. It fuels conflict and may drive valuable employees away, disrupting the cohesion and morale of the entire team.

CHAPTER 5

HEART OF MOTIVATION IS MEANING & PURPOSE: WHY ARE WE HERE?

"There is no power for change greater than a community discovering what it cares about."

– Margaret J. Wheatley

Public service leadership is a collective endeavor, a team sport where success is achieved through shared goals and the collective efforts of every team member. So, the leader's job is to figure out how to bring people together with a drive, so the magic happens. It is as simple as that—creating a sense of purpose and unity among individuals to unleash collective potential and achieve remarkable outcomes. When we find ourselves unable to commit 100 percent, it's often an indicator that we may be involved in the wrong activities or attempting to juggle too many tasks simultaneously. To maintain focus and energy, it becomes crucial to revisit the meaning and purpose behind our actions, ensuring they align with who we aspire to become. This realignment not only sharpens our focus but also fuels commitment and reinforces the unity and purpose necessary for the collective success of the team.

Let us take a step back and talk about our why. Not everyone is naturally inclined to pursue a career in the public sector, and not everyone is suited to thrive in the environment it offers. Regardless of what draws you to local governments, believing in what we do, and the fulfillment derived from adding value and making a difference is the force that fuels passion and binds us together. Make no mistake, only alignment in our values and collective beliefs can keep us steadfast when we face daunting challenges.

Alignment in our "Why" can be the guiding light that reminds us of our purpose and the reason for our commitment to the cause every time it gets dark on us. However, it is trust and respect that enable us to operate as a unified cohesive public service unit. Only in such moments of duty, responsibility, and fulfillment can we endure nuisance. The leader's responsibility is to create an environment that enables building trust and values "respect" to move the needle forward on team performance. So, building a team here is not just about building skill sets and core competencies; it is also about fostering camaraderie and shared values. It is about nurturing a culture where each member buys into the big picture, finds meaning and purpose in what they do, and feels understood, valued, appreciated, supported or empowered to contribute their best. Only in unity and understanding, we find our greatest strength, and only then can perform and drive transformative change. In a public service environment, you can make your team as big as your span allows, with the opportunity for partnership.

Smart and Healthy

Adopting a flexible fluid leadership strategy is key to nurturing adaptability and enhancing organizational performance. Recognizing and adapting to individual variations and needs is essential for both effectiveness and team success. My strategy calls for fostering a supportive team mindset and cultivating a culture of growth, resilience, and shared responsibility. I focused on what I thought were core competencies, building leadership capacity by empowering and leveraging strengths, to enable the team to thrive and adapt to changing circumstances, enhancing overall performance.

My team is currently forming and discovering its dynamics. As a wise lady once told me, "Rome wasn't built in a day." I understand that building an effective team is an ongoing process, requiring careful consideration, intention, and focus. I have both high hopes for the community and faith in my team. We strive because we have to. The unfortunate reality is that there will never be enough resources to meet all the needs. However, this reality propels our team to step up and maximize our efforts to provide a higher standard of service. In doing so, we build a brand and instill confidence in our process.

My overarching goal is for us to become "a smart and healthy" organization, as articulated by Lencioni. This means staying true to our mission and creating a brand that the community can take pride in. Delivering our best is not just an objective but a continuous pursuit. With the right mindset, we can consistently deliver quality in every endeavor. We embrace imperfections and uncertainty. Perfection is an elusive goal, but we can strive to be the best version of ourselves. Despite setbacks, each step we take on this path brings us closer to making a lasting positive impact.

Emphasizing Team mindset

"Great things in business are never done by one person. They're done by a team of people." - Steve Jobs. Throughout our journey in the pursuit of public interest, there will be ups and downs. The team compensates, leans on each other, and keeps commitment and inspiration high. Collaboration enhances completeness as diverse skill sets complement each other, filling gaps and augmenting strengths. Some individuals excel in sprints while others in long distances. Also, the team takes turns, ensuring sustained high energy because there will be times when we are exhausted or not at our best. Those on the bench can save the day.

From a business perspective, embracing a team mindset serves several valuable purposes. It fulfills the fundamental human need for belonging. Meaningful connections are key to motivating from within. When employees feel they are part of a cohesive team, they are more likely to be engaged and motivated. This sense of belonging can lead to job satisfaction and higher performance. No doubt in my mind, individual contributions are critical to the success of the mission. We are all responsible for and capable of impacting our brand. Fostering a team mindset encourages a sense of ownership among employees as contributors. When individuals see themselves as integral parts of a team, they are more inclined to take responsibility for their actions and the outcomes of their projects and input. This ownership mentality leads to better decision-making and a higher level of accountability, which are vital for achieving business goals. This level of investment helps with micro accountability when members hold each other accountable for their contribution. Likewise, a team-oriented approach invites collective pride in outcomes. When employees feel ownership and collaboratively achieve success, they share the sense of accomplishment and can take pride in their collective achievements. This strategy has significant potential for boosting morale, motivation, and overall job satisfaction, leading to a more positive and productive work environment.

CHAPTER 6

ELEVATING PERFORMANCE ADVANTAGE

"I alone cannot change the world, but I can cast a stone across the waters to create many ripples."

– Mother Teresa

Strategic plans end up sitting on shelves for various reasons but mainly for poor alignment with day-to-day operations, poor communication and buy-in from the key stakeholders, and for not having an environment that is conducive for success. To stay ahead of the curve on these issues, first organizations should intentionally cultivate a culture of excellence as a shared value by focusing on growth and on building a culture of leadership and adaptability to align and augment team efforts. This chapter explores the intricacies of fostering growth within organizations, emphasizing investment in an environment for success including the importance of awareness, ongoing development, relationship building, and the creation of effective teams to carry out organizational plans. Success happens when leaders are able to operationalize their vision with a direct line of sight, leaving no room for misunderstanding or mediocrity. And the magic happens when the people fully understand the purpose and their role and take pride in their work. This signifies that the strategies related to the workforce, such as recruitment, development, and engagement, are in complete harmony with the overall objectives and direction of the business. A strategy that puts more weight on attitude and behavior. This alignment ensures that human resources initiatives actively contribute to the success of the broader business strategy. Only then, the people strategy is fully aligned with business strategy.

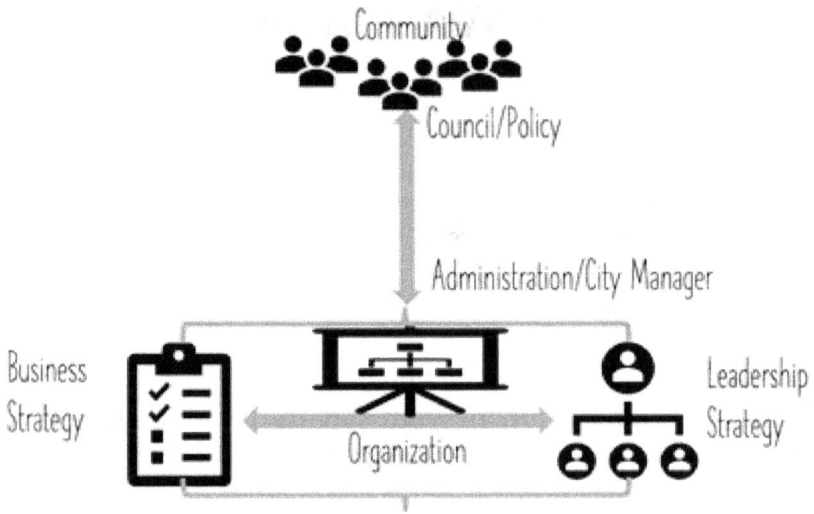

Full Alignment: Community and Organization is Required for the Community to Realize its Full Potential

Adopting a Growth Model

> *"Develop a passion for learning. If you do, you will never cease to grow."*
>
> Anthony J. D'Angelo

In the pursuit of organizational and team success, a fundamental commitment to learning, personal growth, and development is paramount. This commitment involves being intentional about improvement and embracing change as a catalyst for making progress. For effective leadership and team success, a growth mindset must be embedded in concrete policies and opportunities for development and advancement and lived every day. Growth naturally arises through interactions, stress, and challenges, especially when we push our limits. What do you do to help the growth process?

Communication remains the top skill for effective high performing leaders that aids the growth process. "No vision is worth the paper it's printed on unless it is communicated constantly and reinforced with rewards." (Shanmugam, 2021) So, communication is the heart of both the leadership and growth process. It provides clarity and facilitates support and understanding. Good or bad. The right messaging, timeliness, honesty, and constructive criticism are the better choices because the alternative is ignorance, avoidance, neglect, misunderstanding, and resentments.

The city manager, as the *"chief meaning officer" Jack Welch,* builds a small community in the team and helps the team with understanding the "why" and gaining perspective regarding the value of the individual contribution and those incremental adjustments we make every day towards adding value. "A leader's job is to look into the future and see the organization, not as it is, but as it should be. And then help the team see that big picture and understand the "why" and their impact on outcomes.

Effective Leaders are constructive and positive. Choose to see the good in people. We tend to inflate negatives, especially if they touch egos or insecurities. And it is easy to focus on the negative and dwell on the past. Be focused on the future and embrace the reality that no one is perfect. Extend the grace to forgive because mistakes will occur, but they should not mark the end. Leaders are patient, constructive, compassionate, and caring. Decide if it's best to mend and rectify with people. Be kind enough to assist. Sometimes, offer comfort even to those who may seem challenging and completely undeserving.

Leaders set the tone. Adopt a positive outlook. Positive people are more open to change, willing to learn and unlearn, willing to teach, and adaptable to evolving circumstances. This adaptability is a key factor in maintaining productivity and fostering good relationships. Individuals who are positive tend to be more empathetic, understanding, and supportive, creating a conducive atmosphere for healthy relationship building. Setting high standards is also essential for fostering a dynamic and successful work environment. Leave no room for mediocrity. By not tolerating mediocrity, the leader signals a commitment to continuous improvement, innovation, and the pursuit of excellence, ultimately contributing to maintaining a motivated and high-achieving workforce.

Awareness: Emphasis on the Human Element

Part of my leadership strategy lies in fostering a culture of awareness for both leadership development and to facilitate our growth as a team. The system I am introducing, and my approach are a drastic change compared to what the organization is used to. Implementation then requires change management and a generous timeline for the growth process. I delved into my experience fully aware of the fact that nobody likes "change" and not everyone will readily embrace novel approaches. It's a human tendency to not like the discomfort it brings, and we are naturally inclined to avoid pain and the unknown until we trust the process or assured outcomes are favorable and nonthreatening.

Change is uncomfortable because it is perceived to bring pain points. But it is an absolute fact of life and a strategic imperative for those seeking sustained success in an ever-evolving world. If you are not growing and adapting, you need to wake up because you are dying. We succeed when we embrace that fact and when we are able to adapt and bounce back from our setbacks and correct course if need be. I have learned that the most successful teams are the resilient and the committed to continuous learning, adapting to changing circumstances, and those who manage to stay ahead in a constantly changing world.

The advantage truly lies in our capacity to learn and unlearn and in the speed by which we recover, adjust, or pivot. I say unlearn because sometimes we do have to when our beliefs change according to change in perceptions. Some truths are obsolete in light of other better ones. For example, at some point people believed that earth is the center of the universe, which no longer makes sense. I know what you are thinking, some people might still hold those beliefs. Those are the people who are unwilling to unlearn therefore will stay behind. For my team, I continue to emphasize that change is our ally. It is the vehicle through which we can develop, innovate, and grow. My team is encouraged to embrace change as an opportunity to grow and succeed. I know it is easier said than done. So my job is, as a leader, to challenge my team and encourage them to step outside their comfort zone, helping them unlock their untapped capacities. What Patti Seda called in her book *Discovering Job Joy* "Stretching without snapping." I am aware of pain points and the challenges that come with growth and shifting paradigms. But I firmly believe in our ability to reorganize for greater efficiency and achievements.

To facilitate our growth process, I am investing in the principle of awareness as I believe it is the cornerstone of effective teamwork and key to driving higher performance. When team members are aware of each other's communication styles, priorities, and goals, they can collaborate more effectively. An awareness level that supports building and maintaining relationships and helps with understanding and aligning individual efforts with collective goals through enhanced communication and a positive team culture. My goal, ultimately, is to nurture an adaptability culture and to bring the team closer to acknowledging uniqueness, different approaches, and own biases, fostering a collaborative understanding among team members—a pivotal initial stride toward peak performance.

Along with awareness, comes the emphasis on effective communication and prioritizing the well-being and growth of the team as fundamental principles that form the core of my leadership strategy. I believe our chances of success are enhanced when we can effectively understand what helps the team members contribute to our objectives and how we can support each other. MPO assessment was helpful in creating clarity as it gave us the opportunity to learn more about personalities and needs, and to proactively invest in wellbeing for the sustainability of our success. That awareness provides tremendous assistance with effective communication, positioning, and improvement, especially reducing the potential for misunderstanding and with how we can be deliberate about adaptability and tailoring growth and development plans. The most important job you have as a leader is growing your people. (Shanmugam, 2021)

Cognitive bias awareness helps with understanding and recognizing biases that may influence decisions, promoting objectivity and kindness, and creating a culture that challenges preconceptions. Clarity about who we are as a team and acknowledging the diverse strengths and contributions of each team member are key principles that inform direction on our path for success as an organization. Awareness about our own bias helps with walking in others' shoes and helps with equity and looking at things objectively . The value of an individual's contribution is embedded in the collective output of the team, highlighting the interconnectedness and significance of each team member. We strive for social awareness as it contributes to the development of strong positive relationships among team members, ultimately enhancing collaboration and our overall effectiveness. We are an exceptional team when we are thoughtful, fair, and kind.

From a leadership perspective, self-awareness and understanding the dynamics of the team are essential elements in managing the learning, growth, and development process, as well as in fostering positive relationships. Clarity about one's own identity, values, and goals is key for aligning personal aspirations with organizational values, fostering a sense of purpose. i.e. seeing and practicing who you want to be and how that identity fits in with the team and organizational purpose. In a public service context, this awareness forms the foundation for both effective leadership and decision-making.

Also, social awareness plays a critical role in relationship-building. Being attuned to the emotions, perspectives, and needs of others allows the leader to navigate interpersonal dynamics with empathy and understanding. Leaders who possess high emotional intelligence, particularly a strong social awareness, are adept at navigating team dynamics. They have the ability to recognize, understand, manage, and effectively navigate the emotions of others. They can accurately perceive the emotions of their team members and stakeholders. That awareness also enables them to anticipate and address potential issues, fostering a supportive and harmonious work environment. Therefore, they hold an advantage in fostering a collaborative and supportive work environment, demonstrating the ability to recognize, guide, and appreciate the diverse contributions of team members. This skillset works like orchestrating a symphony, where the leader knows how to direct the various elements for optimal performance.

Fostering a culture of awareness includes being intentional about building the capacity to comprehend and respect the emotions, needs, and concerns of others. Understanding allows the team to respond empathetically, adapt their communication style, and cultivate positive and collaborative interactions. As a team, we must be sensitive to and aware of our impact on each other and on the outcomes. Because people are both emotional and rational beings. And sometimes we don't know until we are told. We should be open and approachable enough for people to help that awareness and to figure out what we need to work on as partners and how we organize better for the best outcomes.

The emphasis on awareness and understanding is a major step toward enhancing both teamwork and the overall productive work environment. Recognizing talents, limitations, and interests is instrumental in developing skills, compensating for weaknesses, strategic positioning, and in allowing specialization for optimal outcomes. This approach maximizes productivity, and is also key to managing change, every time "new" is introduced.

Emphasis on Communication

The heart of our process lies in everyone understanding the unique roles each of us plays, the incredible impact of our individual contributions, the power of effective communication, and the emphasis on shared responsibility. I intentionally increased team interactions through a system of touch points and collaborative space that organized our communications and actions. Implementation of Office 365 platform facilitated easy and efficient access and more team collaboration. The Team completely owns our organized "plan of action" that we call the annual work plan. It is important to note that this is in a sense a humanized and animated version of the conventional management information system.

For those who are visual learners, we built in the process of visualizing our work plan for everyone to visually see what is on the table, what's high priority, the accomplishments, and progress. We track, reflect, and discuss our business and status reports through leadership team meeting cadence and reporting structure. We report weekly and monthly for accountability and better management decisions and reports are rolled up quarterly and annually for external communication and celebration. But I put a lot of weight on access for awareness, learning, and for inviting creativity. This level of inclusion provides exposure and invites contribution and learning. We live both growth and pain points together. We celebrate and build off of each other's ideas. We organize and grow together. Besides the strategic plan, the planning process otherwise is lively and very simple. Kaizen style, we start with a target or a desired end state, figure out how we get there, and then watch us get there. When we get there, we stake it and celebrate it. If we fail/fall or hit a setback we get up, discuss why, and figure out how we improve. I know you are thinking, in a public service environment, we get a lot thrown at us. Yes, we respond and address and prioritize those, but we never let them derail our established plans or our decision making process.

In a team-oriented leadership model, individuals support and uplift each other. Seeing progress and accomplishments builds confidence. Discussing opportunities for improvement may be uncomfortable but necessary to ensure success next time. The key is to take ego out of the equation. Every one of us has the capacity to positively influence outcomes, if we are willing to align ourselves with the team's goals and adapt as needed.

It is a leader's responsibility to inspire and guide individuals, influencing their choices and fostering an environment that facilitates their adjustment process. The team builds the plan, is invited to step back and analyze to see the patterns, can elect to contribute ideas, and can influence the plan and provide opinion on accommodations. This level of adaptability, ownership, and investment in a learning environment is technically the essence of both my change management and development strategy.

Building Capacity in the Team

"There is almost no limit to the potential of an organization that recruits good people, raises them up as leaders and continually develops them."

-John Maxwell

Building on strength unlocks untapped capacity within individuals and teams. Focus adds more capacity. And the process of practical learning maximizes potential. It can be painful but stress molds individuals into leadership. Throughout my career I hired a lot of people for different roles. My approach has now evolved to favor hiring for potential and grit because I learned that productivity requires discipline and commitment. Now, I don't put much weight on experience, rather I look for intelligence and potential with the right attitude, of course. In order to achieve high levels of productivity, we must cultivate discipline, which involves consistent effort, focus, and adherence to a set of tasks or goals. Discipline ensures that one stays on track, meets deadlines, and follows through on commitments. Commitment is equally essential; it fuels the perseverance needed to overcome challenges and setbacks. Without discipline and commitment, achieving sustained productivity becomes a daunting task, making these qualities fundamental to success in any endeavor.

Managing a team is mostly about positioning, leveraging strengths, and supporting or compensating for weaknesses. To create a well-rounded high-performance team, it is essential to recognize that everyone has areas where they excel and areas where they may struggle. The manager's role is to optimize team interactions and dynamics, leading to a more productive and harmonious work environment, while helping individuals reach their full potential. This approach recognizes that every individual on a team has a unique set of abilities, interests, and areas where they may need assistance or development.

With full awareness and understanding of individual qualities, interests, and needs, every team member can potentially present their best contribution, adding exceptional value to team outcomes. Through discovery and empowerment, team members learn where to invest their energy and are encouraged to employ their passion and focus on their natural strengths. It is ok to learn from trial and error, with the appropriate oversight.

By concentrating efforts on areas of proficiency, individuals can maximize their potential. They can't learn how to drive in a parked car. Stress and challenges serve as opportunities to shape leadership qualities. The pressure and demands inherent in such situations provide a platform for individuals to demonstrate and develop their leadership skills. However, it's important to note that the process of learning and growth can be challenging and even painful at times, as it often involves stepping outside the comfort zone and confronting new and demanding situations. It is important for leaders to know that they are not there to impose how team members do their jobs. They are there to facilitate and offer advice and support.

Where's the Leader?

Individual characteristics exist on a spectrum. People vary in terms of agreeableness, tolerance, conscientiousness, and assertiveness. Some people are generalists who prefer and are very good at seeing the big picture and some are specialists who are technical experts by nature. Some are very adaptable, and they can excel with a diversity of tasks and some are not so much, they would rather focus on one task at a time to deliver flawless results. Developing and enhancing skill sets must be tailored to individual needs. Simply recognizing and respecting these differences and understanding how to address or compensate for weaknesses while offering support enables effectiveness. Remember your job as leader is to be wherever the team needs you. Sometimes forefront, having the teams' back for support, alongside assisting or holding hands, or in the trenches if need be.

The Leader is Where the Team Needs Them

You have to know when and how to lead the team. For instance, individuals inclined towards agreeableness may struggle with conflict and saying no. This comes from being inherently compassionate and caring. Acknowledging this aspect of their character and learning how to compensate for it is crucial for fulfilling your role as their leader and for their skill development. The last thing you want for those exceptional people is to burn out filling everyone's bucket and neglecting their wellbeing. Some people can use assurance and encouragement more than others. Some may need a reality check to help them see things objectively. Build the relationship that allows for having hard conversations otherwise, there will be confrontations, stress, and conflict.

While I appreciate initiative and individual strengths, I have always honored fairness and equal opportunity to level the playing field. Because not everyone on the team had the opportunity to have experience in leadership, my core leadership competencies include effective decision making, care, kindness, and ability to manage complexities. Leaders reveal themselves when they remain steadfast and take charge when faced with adversity, pressure, and challenge. Everyone on the team is provided with the opportunity to shine. "To be Clear, Capacity building is not about doing more. It is about doing more of the right things. (Glazer, 2019). This is true because my organization, by design, is run by the best idea rather than by hierarchy.

Heart of Engagement: Empower

It is a common tendency for people to be motivated or influenced by their own vested interests. This means that they are more likely to make decisions and take actions that align with their personal gains. Understanding and acknowledging those natural aspects of human behavior led me to lean on an empowerment approach that involved empowering functional leaders to take ownership of their functions. Ownership creates strong incentives for leaders to be invested in the success of their functions. The prospect of receiving credit for positive outcomes serves as both motivation and a source of inspiration, while also functioning as a caution against potential failures. This approach fosters commitment, resulting in a more engaged and proactive team.

Responsibility, ownership, and accountability are interconnected concepts. Responsibility is the initial acceptance of a task, ownership is the personal investment in its success, and accountability is the commitment to answer for the results. Together, they create a powerful framework for reliability and commitment. Those who take ownership are not just completing a task; they are personally invested in its successful outcome. Accountability ties responsibility and ownership together. When individuals are accountable, they not only fulfill their responsibilities but also answer for the results. In a sense, accountability is the bridge that connects responsibility and ownership to measurable outcomes. It implies answerability for the consequences, whether they are positive or negative.

For full engagement, empower leaders to take responsibility and own their functions, clarify acknowledgement, and help with the accountability process. Through this participatory approach to leadership, my function leaders and I partner in a constructive and productive relationship. My vision for our relationship is to be reciprocal, productive, and generous.

> *"It's amazing what you can accomplish when you don't care who gets the credit."*
>
> — Harry Truman

Adaptability: Be sensitive to needs to build capacity.

Fear holds people back from realizing their full potential, especially fear of humiliation. It is irrational at times and can be totally paralyzing. But dreams are on the other side of fear and growth only happens when we are outside our comfort zone. When we introduce workplace change as part of a vision implementation, it is equally important to account for the potential emotional impacts. Managing the psychological impact of change is often overlooked or made too simple. I would emphasize taking a soft transformative approach. My approach has been making incremental changes to ensure a seamless transition, while creating an environment where courage, kindness, grace, consistency, and adaptability flourish, paving the way for the team's success. I am here with an unobstructed vision, direction, and support. I believe magic happens when individuals come together as a harmonious community, each person contributing their unique strengths and valuable perspective. As a leader, I believe in nurturing the best in everyone, unlocking hidden talents, and inspiring them to make decisions that benefit the collective.

Develop Negotiation Skills

Team leadership is mostly a facilitation of process. Effective facilitation often boils down to the leader's negotiation skills. Leaders need strong negotiation skills to navigate diverse perspectives, resolve disputes, and influence positive outcomes. While negotiation skills are frequently acclaimed for their value in business and for serving as a crucial element in making successful deals, I find these skills equally important at times of conflict and difficulty, when parties find themselves at opposing ends. They are even more basic and ordinary in community than in business. Conflict happens when two people don't believe the same thing. Whenever we are dealing with people, we'll end up negotiating. If you want to be a successful leader, you have got to master or sharpen your negotiation skills.

Awareness and the ability to identify common ground and appeal to both ethos and logos are instrumental in achieving success. In a nutshell, the most successful leaders happen to be great negotiators. They can navigate complex situations, build positive productive relationships, and achieve successful outcomes in various professional and personal contexts. Here's a couple of skills I observed and felt that they are proven valuable. I did not invent any of it. I just happen to recognize and appreciate them. I know success when I see it. Make no mistake, they are all useful. But being an effective communicator and being creative and adaptable is what is going to get you there.

Active Listening: Paying close attention to the other party's perspective, needs, and concerns. Please note that understanding the situation and the root cause of the problem is half of the solution.

Effective Communication: Clearly articulating your position, expectations, and desired outcomes. This should be your top skill. You have to be able to adapt to their style to get your point through. I know it takes two to tango. But, trust me, you are not effective, and you will go nowhere if you are unable to connect or can't make your point.

Empathy: Understanding and acknowledging the emotions and motivations of the other party. If you don't understand people, you don't understand business, period. People will be people. And they are mostly emotional beings.

Problem Solving Approach: Approaching negotiations as a collaborative problem-solving process to find mutually beneficial solutions. Attitude is the most critical aspect of your negotiation skills. The other party needs to feel that your intent is constructive. Let it be.

Adaptability: Being flexible and open to adjusting your approach based on the evolving dynamics of the negotiation. In my experience, negotiations are very dynamic. Sometimes the solution is in the willingness to give and take. This is the trickiest skill. Remember, timing is key. You can't reason when people are emotional. You have to meet emotion with emotion to properly de-escalate. You can come back to reasoning once emotions settle.

Patience: building capacity for patience is the hardest thing I ever had to do. Remaining calm and composed, especially in challenging or lengthy negotiations. The last thing you want is to show your impatience. It backfires.

Building Rapport: Establishing a positive relationship and rapport with the other party, fostering a cooperative atmosphere. Nothing prevents you from having a very respectful relationship with your worst enemy. You should be able to make simple connections. Trust me, we are all humans with needs. This skill helps with building capacity for respect and trust. This should be easy for kind people. Manage your emotions. Choose to be kind, always Don't ever let other people define who you are.

Assertiveness: Advocate for your needs and interests without being overly aggressive. Remain calm and composed. Bear in mind, you don't have to act aggressively. But you should have the capacity for aggression. Sometimes you need it.

Conflict Resolution: Effectively managing and resolving conflicts that may arise during negotiations. Things can escalate during negotiations. You have to have the capacity to address. Know when to retract and kindly offer a resolution. There's a lot of character and integrity in those situations. Learn how to read the room. Don't waste your time. There are situations that aren't worth wasting your breath. Learn how to embrace failure. Nothing scares me more than someone who's unwilling to learn. Unfortunately. in a public service environment, you will meet those a lot.

Strategic Thinking: Approach negotiations with a strategic mindset, anticipating potential scenarios, concessions, and considering both short-term and long-term goals. You do not want to be short sighted. Because you could get yourself out of a situation creating a problem later. Think creatively to explore alternative solutions that satisfy both parties' interests. Just try to be open-minded. Think outside the box.

CHAPTER 7

BUILDING LEADERSHIP CAPACITY

"Trust is the glue of life. It's the most essential ingredient in effective communication. It's the foundational principle that holds all relationships."

—Stephen R. Covey

Emotions play a crucial role in shaping perceptions, fundamentally influencing behaviors and interactions. I would say trust is about feeling safe. It is so basic that it is second to physiological needs, according to Maslo's hierarchy of needs. In the workplace it is the most fundamental prerequisite for productive collaboration and effective relationships. Lack of trust poses the risk of undermining team health and therefore organizational productivity. When we don't trust someone, it means we are somewhat sure that something bad is going to happen to us with a degree of certainty. Why is this important? In absence of trust, we calculate our moves, take an adversarial posture, overthink, and overanalyze everything. We end up being on our guard 100% of the time. We withdraw, limit our interactions, or worse yet attack before we get attacked because of the horror story we told ourselves that the other party is out to get us. Those stories are destructive. It is not a productive relationship nor is it an environment for success. The team is then contaminated, stressed out, dysfunctional, and wasteful. The hostile environment stresses out those compassionate and caring members and drives talented people away and wastes energy and resources on conflicts.

How do you build trust? Being intentional about building trust is proactive and essential for team success. It's established through leadership building, open communication, consistency, transparency, and ethical behavior, leading to a belief in good faith and meeting expectations. We don't trust the people we don't know because the possibilities are infinite and tend to trust those we know. Consistency in our responses to stimuli allows people to understand us. It provides insight into our decision-making process and enables them to predict our reactions. This consistency fosters the building of trust and comfort in relationships.

To build trust, leaders need to lead with integrity and to be reliable, transparent, communicative, and consistent throughout both easy and tough times. They need to be authentic, honest, and clear about their intentions, sharing information openly and addressing concerns promptly. Being open about our intentions, decisions, and even our mistakes helps foster the building of trust. Clarity about expectations and addressing concerns through hard conversations and coaching helps with elevating relationships.

Leaders should also encourage a culture of leadership and kindness, emphasizing ideal virtues. We tend to trust people who are kind and despise those who we think are cruel and manipulative. Being kind and supportive projects safety and is an indicator that you are a good person who is most likely to treat people fairly. That in itself is assuring because it takes that risk of not knowing what's going to happen away. Tolerance and being intentional about adapting to other people's communication styles and sensitive to their needs show respect and build comfort in the relationship. Being authentic with the team demonstrates your humanity. No one is perfect. Embracing imperfection and committing to being constructive builds comfort in the relationships.

They should also adopt a positive outlook and encourage positivity and integrity. When individuals consistently approach challenges and interactions with a positive future-oriented perspective, that builds trust within the team because the approach is constructive. This is especially true when the leader engages in conflict fairly. It's inevitable that conflict will arise. The team will be watching how the leader addresses the situation and will form their perception and drive their own value based on how the leader treats the parties involved.

Building a Culture of Leadership: Emphasizing Ideal Virtues

"The best way to spot an idiot is to look for the person who is cruel. Empathy and compassion are evolved states of being. They require the mental capacity to step past our most primal urges".

J.B. Pritzker.

According to Pritzker, our initial thoughts often stem from fear or judgment, a product of evolutionary survival instincts. To be kind, we must consciously divert our minds from these primal urges to overcome our innate, suspicious instincts, embracing a more evolved mindset. Kindness is a cherished value that forms the bedrock of the organizational culture I aspire to. I encourage the team to be kind to one another and treat everyone with respect. It is crucial to acknowledge that none of us have complete insight into everything that is happening in people's lives. Therefore, upholding kindness remains of utmost importance in all our interactions with our team members. I want them to treat others the way they want to be treated. None of us want to be the straw that broke the camel's back. While respect is a non-negotiable expectation, it is essential to show empathy and understanding to our team members as we all adjust to new processes or roles. As leaders in public service, we model those virtues. People tend to reciprocate and may feel obligated to pay it forward. By fostering an environment of kindness, we create a supportive community where people feel valued and motivated to give their best, even during challenging times.

Discipline & Grit

"A river cuts through rock, not because of its power, but because of its persistence."

— Jim Watkins

Never underestimate the power of persistence. Grit is persevering and maintaining passion and effort despite facing challenges and setbacks. This quality holds immense value in the public sector and should be nurtured, developed and practiced. Leaders with grit anchor their teams by staying committed to their mission. Resilience, a core aspect of grit, proves crucial in navigating the intricate landscape of leadership, especially within the complexities of public service. For leaders dealing with long-term objectives and controversial issues, grit becomes a defining factor. The ability to stay committed to goals over the long term, even amidst adversity, is what sets successful leaders apart.

Cultivating grit in teams involves fostering a mindset and developing habits that enable individuals to persist and maintain effort. The strategies I am focusing on besides the growth mindset are: defining clear and meaningful goals that resonate with team values, remaining positive and in touch with our purpose "Why", focusing on opportunities in setbacks because it helps when we focus on the bright side, managing stress, and building a support system. It is not easy to face criticism on a global scale. I believe maintaining a positive outlook, focusing on what we can control, and influence is also key. We can't control the world around us but we can control how we react to it. Some people tend to internalize negative feedback. In fact, no one likes feedback. What you do with that feedback varies. Developing a thicker skin and learning how to compartmentalize is key to their development. Honestly, mastering the art of managing one's emotions and compartmentalization is essential for leadership skills development. For instance, individuals often internalize criticism, but it's crucial for you as a leader to help your team recognize that others' perceptions don't shape their identity. Because it has the potential for shaking one's confidence. "You may not control all the events that happen to you, but you can decide not to be reduced by them" Maya Angelo.

> *"Discipline is doing what you hate to do,*
> *but do it like you love it."*
>
> — Mike Tyson

Discipline provides the structure and focus necessary for day-to-day operations while grit empowers both the leaders and their team to persevere through challenges and work towards long-term objectives. Together, these attributes contribute to the resilience and success of leaders in a dynamic environment. As Denzel Washington puts it: "On the road to achieving your dreams apply discipline and consistency. Because without discipline you'll never start and without consistency you'll never finish." As I mentioned at the beginning of this book, success is never an accident. Being intentional about leadership and building the right system for collective growth is the how and consistency is the secret. I am emphasizing that throughout our growth journey as a community, we do not confuse movement with progress and remember the power of courage, kindness, consistent effort, and caring for the people around us. Only we can limit ourselves. We practice who we want to be. That's how we get there. These qualities will not only help us navigate transitions smoothly but also elevate and position us for greater success in fulfilling our purpose in the face of an ever-changing landscape.

Courage And Humility

Leaders are courageous and humble. "I have learned over the years that when one's mind is made up, this diminishes fear; knowing what must be done does away with fear." Rosa Parks. Courage is the ability to act despite your fear, standing at the core of effective decision-making and expression. It encompasses the willingness to step outside the comfort zone, confront obstacles, and uphold principles even in the face of potential risks. Throughout my professional and personal journey, I've been fortunate to learn from exceptional leaders who shared a common attribute – courage. This virtue, more than any other, has garnered my utmost admiration. I believe it's through facing adversity that my character has been truly shaped and strengthened. Effective leaders are courageous. They carry themselves with the confidence of a lion. Unstoppable, they address challenges head-on. They have the courage to trust people, even though there is always the risk of being let down. In order to do so you have to have confidence in your ability to address potential impacts. They are not afraid to be in the trenches or to put their foot down taking a stance, unapologetically. They must have the courage to take the initiative, have a difficult conversation, admit when they are wrong, and most importantly have the courage to live with being disliked. Not everyone will agree with their decisions. But that is what they were hired for.

To see what others fail to see. They are not in business to be liked. And that is why they need to be great communicators and trustworthy and must be of integrity. Honestly, if you stand for something, it is impossible to please everyone. Leaders do their best to drive the point home, explaining, arguing, justifying, and managing emotional reactions. But they also must be able to stand their ground and be ok with being disliked. Be courageous and encourage your team to do the same by instilling a mindset and creating an environment for developing the skills that enable them to confront challenges, take risks, and act with resilience. You can practice who you want to be. Your core character is built through a pattern of your behavior. Building strong character means encouraging consistency in showing courage. "Character is how you show up on your worst day" Adam Grant

> *"A leader's job is to shepherd, not necessarily to always shine. It's about the mission, the team, and the tribe, not about you and your ego. Leaders today should be more conductors than solo artists."*
>
> — Brad Lomenick H3 Leadership

Ego is the enemy of collective growth. Humility fosters an environment where others are willing to listen and engage positively. Humility is regarded as one of the most important leadership qualities. (Nelson Mandela). When you approach others with humility, making it clear that you pose no threat, people are more likely to welcome you and be receptive to what you have to say. It is a human tendency to fear the unknown. Employees will try and do their best if the environment is enabling. In an atmosphere of courage and humility, we can navigate change rationally and more effectively and embrace the opportunities it brings. This also must be coupled with trust and the utility of psychological safety. The team needs to feel that their leader will be there to support them when things go wrong. It is the leader's responsibility and duty to have their back. I am investing in reaching a state where individuals trust my process and feel seen, understood, supported, and protected or safe from humiliation and retribution. I wanted my team to be able to share their ideas, thoughts, and concerns without fear of judgment. Only in such an environment, innovation and outside the box solutions happen. I was introduced as "change". You can imagine the uncertainty that preceded my arrival and occupied staff minds. That was my baseline. I worked with that. I had to build relationships, assurance, understanding, and confidence in my decision-making process.

Change and life, for that matter, demand a flexible and adaptable mindset. My strategy is about fostering a culture of support where everyone understands the importance of adaptability, where they feel safe to try and learn from their experiences. Learning is part of the process. We are all learning to push our limits. It is about recognizing that we all have a role to play in shaping outcomes and growth and success are on the other side of our fears.

Building Learning Muscle is Gaining Advantage

"Only those who dare to fail greatly can ever achieve greatly."

- Robert F. Kennedy.

Helping team members reach their full potential is an investment in their growth that benefits both the individuals and the organization. Creating a culture infused with awareness, gratitude, support, kindness, and a dedication to continuous improvement, alongside a team mindset and psychological safety, establishes an environment conducive to satisfaction and high performance. By promoting a growth mindset and being intentional about fostering a culture of learning, the team can actively build their learning muscle, resulting in a more agile, adaptive, and high-performing collective. I am excited for the incredible heights we will reach together. The path ahead might have its challenges, but with each other by our side, we are unstoppable. With persistence, we will be able to say it loudly, by our actions, that we are a high performing organization.

Coaching is helping people see what they do not see. The city manager plays a crucial role as a coach to their leadership team. Just like a sports coach who knows their players' strengths and weaknesses, a city manager should have a deep understanding of their team members and how to position them effectively to maximize overall team performance. Knowing your players requires awareness and involves recognizing the individual skills, expertise, ambitions, and talents of each member of the leadership team. This understanding allows the city manager as a leader to create a well-rounded team that can address challenges and opportunities. It also enables them to make informed decisions about task delegation, project assignments, and team composition.

Positioning team members for maximum performance is aligning their roles and responsibilities with their strengths and interests. This not only enhances individual job satisfaction but also increases overall team productivity. For instance, if a team member excels in analytics, they may be better suited for budget-related tasks, while someone with effective communication skills could lead public outreach efforts. We all have unique talents and at different levels of efficiency when it comes to performing a task, communicating, using our imagination to produce something out of the ordinary.

To maximize productivity, it is essential to ensure that we are harnessing the full potential of our team members by enabling them to work primarily in environments that align with their strengths and preferences. For instance, introverted individuals tend to thrive in quieter settings so they should be provided the opportunity to withdraw and recharge while extroverted people gain energy from being around people.

Agreeable risk averse team members complement those pioneers with a higher need to win personalities. Navigating team dynamics, however, is a tough endeavor because people are complex, emotional, and can be unpredictable. Improving team performance requires more than coaching and positioning. It involves connecting with and emotionally supporting people. It is hard to deliver feedback if you have not already established a good relationship with your employees. Leaders deal with challenges and emotions that come up along the way and drama caused by variations on team personality characteristics. They spend a great deal of time smoothing egos and confronting negative thoughts, requiring a blend of skillfulness, stamina, and patience to handle those challenges effectively. Undealt with emotions do not magically disappear. Conflict delayed is conflict multiplied,creating more issues. The most prominent and dangerous ones are burnout and the buildup of micro disappointments. Undealt with, those can potentially undermine team health and therefore organizational productivity. A whole side of leadership that manifests itself in character and integrity to be able handle some situations, speaking forcefully but with compassion and genuine care.

Gaining a competitive advantage is essential for long-term viability and prominence. When team members feel psychologically safe, they are more likely to contribute their best ideas, collaborate effectively, and take calculated risks to drive innovation and growth without fear of negative consequences. The leader plays a crucial role in fostering this safety. They should not only empower their team when they are willing and ready but also be prepared to support them when things go wrong. Things will go wrong. Because falling is part of the growth process. Building that environment involves acknowledging and accepting the fact that humans make mistakes and embracing failures as opportunities for growth. And requires care, open communication, and team support.

"It's when things go wrong that we learn the most."

— Simon Sinek.

Therefore, we commit to continuous improvement, and we take notes. Leaders should build a culture of continuous improvement. The most effective teams tend to be the most adaptable. This means regularly evaluating team processes and following team dynamics closely, making necessary adjustments, and learning from both successes and failures. This is a culture of awareness and adaptability. An organization's ability to learn, and translate that learning into action rapidly, is the ultimate competitive advantage. (Shanmugam, 2021).

Take away

Leadership is about fostering a culture of trust and support while helping individuals and the team reach their full potential. Effective leaders understand that there is no one-size-fits-all approach, and they adapt their leadership style to the needs of their team and the demands of the situation. Readiness to address challenges head-on comes from understanding the dynamics of change management. Success requires paying attention to organizational health and a strong commitment to growth, consistent effort, and adaptability to meet our evolving needs.

Leadership Strategy outline:

1. Not a one-size fits all. Be aware of the needs of the situation.

2. Know your team.

3. Combine vision, adaptability, team support and empowerment, and a determination to overcome challenges.

4. Adopt a growth mindset to improve performance and productivity.

5. Focus on maximizing resources and building confidence in the team's capabilities.

6. Commit to nurturing the team and helping them grow without overwhelming them, through a balanced and thoughtful approach. Inspire, impower, expose,

7. Help the team understand that they complement each other and with their fulfillment journey.

8. Emphasize ideal virtues.

9. Remember the difference between battle and war.

10. After action review: a culture of awareness, reflection, and continuous improvement

11. Be ready to live in a fishbowl.

12. Adopting a team mindset not only fulfills the need for belonging but also promotes a sense of ownership and fosters pride in outcomes. These elements can contribute to a healthier and more productive workplace. In challenging times, a team-led approach ensures resilience. Leaders motivate and guide the team through difficulties, drawing on the collective spirit to overcome obstacles.

13. Coach your team. Understand each team member's capabilities and strategically position them to optimize team performance. A leader's role in an organization is to create an environment that facilitates growth and development by empowering their team members, providing support, and encouraging them to push beyond their comfort zones. This approach can lead to exceptional performance and personal growth within the team.

14. Optimize productivity through recognizing and accommodating the unique strengths and preferences of team members. By doing so, the leader creates an environment where each member can perform at their best, leading to improved job satisfaction, collaboration, and overall effectiveness.

15. Pay it forward: Leadership is the responsibility to see those around you rise. Be intentional about inspiring, empowering, and exposing your team to learning and experience. They cannot learn how to drive in a parked car. Give them the keys and your guidance. Stress focusses their attention and sharpens their skills.

16. Growth is a fundamental aspect of effective leadership. Learn how to nurture the development of your team members. This involves providing opportunities for learning, skill-building, and advancement. A great leader recognizes and cultivates the potential in others, helping them reach their full potential. It is their job to create an environment for growth and development. This involves empowering individuals rather than micromanaging them. You do not hire a talent and then do their job for them. Leaders are teachers. They should stand behind their team members, offering encouragement and guidance when necessary. Their role is to draw out greatness from

their team by providing the necessary tools, mentorship, and opportunities for growth. This support can take the form of pushing individuals beyond their comfort zones, as it is often in these challenging situations that the most significant personal and professional development occurs. Sometimes, people do not realize their full potential until they are placed in demanding roles, backed by a leader who believes in their abilities and provides them with words of encouragement and support. By trusting and encouraging their team, leaders inspire confidence and help individuals reach heights they might not have thought possible.

17. Public sector leaders must be able to navigate opposition and challenges, both from within the organization and from external stakeholders. Decisions may be faced with resistance, requiring leaders to engage in effective communication and negotiation.

18. ***Benefits of recognizing and accommodating employees' preferences:***

    Optimal Performance: *When team members are in their "stimulation zone," where the environment matches their working style, they are more likely to perform at their best.*

    Enhanced Job Satisfaction: *Allowing individuals to work in environments that suit their preferences can lead to increased job satisfaction. When people are comfortable in their work settings, they are happier and more engaged.*

    Improved Collaboration: *Combining the strengths of different team members can lead to better outcomes. Introverts excel at detailed analysis and planning, while* *extroverts thrive in roles that involve networking and communication.*

Reduced Stress: *Being in an environment that aligns with one's preferences can reduce stress levels. This, in turn, can lead to better mental well-being and overall job performance.*

Increased Innovation: *A diverse team that operates in environments suited to individual preferences can foster innovation by bringing different perspectives and ideas to the table.*

How will I know if I am successful in building leadership?

Leadership is knowing when to step up when it is the time to step up and take charge. It is knowing what to do when things are uncertain, complicated, and hard, and knowing where to be for your team, front leading the way, by their side to assist, in the trenches doing it together, or in the back for support and encouragement.

I will know I have succeeded when I can take comfort knowing my team got this and they are not going to let the team down. I encourage my team to step out of their comfort zone and up to take the initiative. I believe we grow into leadership in proportion to the weight of responsibility we are willing to take. It is a capacity we gain only through stress and going through hardship. We cannot develop leadership otherwise. The environment I am creating will bring out the leader in those who are up to it and that's the legacy I am leaving behind.

How do you know if you are a leader? Leadership is not about a title but rather about the positive impact and influence you have on those around you. When others look to you for guidance or are inspired by your actions, you are a leader. You are a leader when you can effectively communicate ideas, motivate others, and understand and empathize with the needs and concerns of others. When you can bounce back from setbacks and encourage others to do the same. You are a leader when others willingly follow your guidance, when your actions inspire and influence positive change, and when you take responsibility for the well-being and development of those around you. Leadership is evidenced not in titles but in the impact you have on people and the direction you guide them toward. If you find yourself inspiring others, fostering collaboration, and navigating challenges with resilience, you truly embody the qualities of a leader.

CHAPTER 8

MAKING HARD DECISIONS

"It takes a great deal of courage to stand up to your enemies, but even more to stand up to your friends."

—J.K. Rowling

Budgeting is an art but in the public sector, fiscal year planning is becoming more of a "dare to make it" exercise. The following conversation happened between two characters in a show called "Suits" written by Aaron Korsh. The characters Harvey and Donna had a tense conversation, which resonated with me during budget time, dealing with the unfunded mandates and the impact of HF718, a property tax reform policy. Harvey and I are the same when it is budget time. A dialogue in my head between council and myself and the tension revolved around budget cuts, representing the situation to a tee.

Donna: "Why are you attacking me? I am not the enemy."

Harvey: "You sure as hell right now."

Donna: "What? Why am I..."

Harvey: "Because I am getting ready for a fight, and you're telling me that you don't think I can win."

Donna: "I am not telling you that. I am telling you I am petrified."

Harvey: "And I understand, but I don't have time to comfort you."

Donna: "Well, I need you to make time."

Harvey: "And I can't."

Donna: "HARVEY, THIS IS MY LIFE."

Harvey: "The thought of you going to prison makes me want to drop to my knees. You want to hear me say it? There it is. But That's not 'gonna' happen because I am not going to let it happen. But in order to do that, you need to let me do what I do."

Donna: "Harvey."

Harvey: "THAT'S ENOUGH! You want someone to give you a hug, go to Lewis. You want someone to get you 'outta' this thing, you need to leave me alone."

Just to provide some context, after having many tense conversations we managed to secure a balanced budget, this time around. It did come, however, with a few discontented community partners and a very cautious spending plan. My focus remains on the long game, where sustainability takes precedence over short-term gratification every time.

Balancing the city's financial well-being amidst pressing demands is a dance that demands thoughtful deliberation. As the custodian of the city's financial health, I grapple with the challenge of addressing community and organizational needs within the constraints of a tight budget. In this chapter, let us talk about the strategies I took to navigate this delicate balance between progress and fiscal responsibility and provide insights into the proactive steps taken to harmonize financial prudence with the imperative of addressing the pressing needs of our community.

Show me your budget and I will tell you who you are.

My approach to budgeting involves orchestrating rigorous budget planning sessions with the team, delving into cost-saving measures, judicious allocation of resources, and actively seeking opportunities to maximize outcomes. The prime focus was on ensuring resources were timely aligned with our overarching priorities. Priority-based budgeting, in particular, resonates with me more than any other exercise. It is my Ikigai (KIZUNA, 2022), my source of joy and purpose. Unlike the private sector, government budgeting takes on a whole new dimension, resembling the challenge of solving a complex riddle with the ever-present influence of politics, poised to derail reason at any moment. In Iowa, the city budget is dictated by the State's code "document of limitations". The authority to tax is given to us through a delegation of police power from state government to local governments. The State will always make sure we don't overstay our welcome. As we assemble budgets to fund community programs and services, the State code and guidelines outline the specifics of how revenues are collected, allocated, and spent.

The budget is also the single most important council decision, as the authorized budget serves as a crucial tool, providing the necessary resources to sustain and improve city service levels. "Don't tell me what you value. Show me your budget and I will tell you what you value". (Biden) Basically, your budget is your statement. I still remember my professor from graduate college, who supervised my field problem project and taught me resources economics, emphasizing that actual sales data is the truest and indisputably superior to survey data. According to him, sales data unveil the actual level of interest people have in a commodity. Our discussions back then revolved around housing location choices, and I was working on estimating and isolating the value of a neighborhood (the location) to the buyers relative to the purchasing price. He argued that unlike hypothetical scenarios where one may overvalue or undervalue something, housing sales data reflect real decisions. It reveals how much people were willing to pay for the commodity. In a survey if you ask the question, they give you an estimate without the consequences. But if they have gone through the choice of buying the house, they actually faced the decision and the consequence of that decision to settle their willingness to pay at a price that met the market supply. I couldn't agree more. What you are able to accommodate in a tight budget reveals your priorities and how well you follow your budget guidelines reveals a lot about you and shows your discipline, will power, and your level of fiscal responsibility.

Ideally, the budget process would start with a strategic planning process to identify priorities, making sure everyone is on the same page regarding priorities, to make sure we are aligning resources with the city's goals, needs, and long-term policy. Budget includes revenues and expenditures forecasts and allocations according to funding rules and guidelines. Typical revenue sources are property tax, sales tax, utility enterprises, and user and franchise fees. This prolonged process of planning ends with the adoption of a schedule of spending for improvements classified according to the chart of accounts and rolls up to government functions. These are public works, public safety, culture & recreation, community & economic development, and general government. That is the format that the state specified. The adoption of that schedule authorizes resources such as collection of property taxes, provides a basis for utility rate increases and establishes direction for the upcoming fiscal year, in terms of services provided to the community.

Because there are many stakeholders involved in the process and before I dive in, I make sure we all have established our agreed upon budget development guidelines. In Oskaloosa my fiscal year 2024 & 25 budget development guidelines were:

1. Present a balanced and sustainable budget that aids long-term sustainability.

2. Conservative revenue and expenditure forecasts to ensure and maintain financial health.

3. Maintain a healthy general fund reserve >35%, with a four-to-six-month operating reserve to support security & creditworthiness.

4. Fund Capital Improvement Plan in the most equitable and fiscally responsible way.

5. Enhance service delivery serving community sustainability.

Because of its impact, budgeting is a fundamental responsibility of the City Manager role. It is like creating a roadmap, charting the course for expenditures and revenue generation. I have treated both fiscal year 2024 and fiscal year 2025 budgets differently because fiscal year 2024 was the first opportunity for full alignment with the strategic plan while feeling the compounded impact of property tax reform that sets in for fiscal year 2025, with House File 718 being in full effect. I approached budget planning with meticulous attention to context, considering the priorities, and aspirations of the community. Before we begin we start with a comprehensive review of the city's financial standing.

With a fresh eye and like a seasoned auditor, I scrutinized the cost recovery model, analyzed expenditure patterns, and assessed long-term financial obligations and projects in the pipeline against capacity. This level of analysis provided a solid foundation for informed decision-making and helped identify areas where cost-saving measures or new cost allocation models could be implemented to optimize service and maximize value, while maintaining financial health. After wrapping up the strategic planning development process, allocations and cost recovery was my first step towards the start of remodeling our business model.

Exploring cost-saving measures has become a critical component of our budgeting and control strategy. My team engaged in zero-base budgeting examining each expenditure item, evaluating its necessity, efficiency, and potential for optimization. Like thrifty shoppers, we sought ways to maximize benefits and reduce costs with the intent of delivering the quality service the community deserves. Contracts reviews and renegotiating vendor agreements were among the approaches we adopted. I realized some deals must be revisited however, overtime. Government process takes time and my approach to change has been "administered over time". The last thing I want is to shock the system. But I believe by leveraging the city's credibility and buying power, we should be able to secure favorable terms and lower costs for essential goods and services.

Collaboration with neighboring entities and the county will play a crucial role in our cost-saving efforts. We explored opportunities for shared services and joint procurement, leveraging economies of scale and our purchasing power to achieve cost efficiencies. Pooling resources and expertise, we should be able to provide high-quality services, while minimizing financial strain. Both the city and the county need to honor this strategy as we need it more than ever.

In addition to cost-saving measures, we actively pursued grant opportunities to maximize resources. Grants are financial lifelines, providing additional funding for projects and initiatives. Some projects were possible only because of grant opportunities.

Part of this strategy is to commit to conducting thorough research, identifying grants that aligned with our priorities and needs. My team and I worked closely with community partners to develop competitive grant proposals, highlighting the city's needs and potential for positive impact. We continue to pursue funding for our community projects such as major road construction, wastewater treatment plant additional capacity, brownfields redevelopment, parks, and stormwater projects. We were successful in landing a couple community ones and a couple of major ones through our Federal representative office and State IDOT, IFA and IEDA. Hopefully, we will continue to gain traction and remain in the spotlight.

Securing grants requires surveys, studies, plans, and ensuring that we carefully followed guidelines and requirements, highlighting the city's needs, community engagement efforts, and expected outcomes. These grant funds allow us to implement vital projects that would have otherwise been financially challenging and burdening. Reaching out to elected officials and community partners engaging them through our visioning process and in our struggles helped push the needle through and opened doors otherwise we are not able to go through.

Maintaining the city's financial stability while balancing growth and maintenance demands is a delicate dance. We carefully evaluated capital investments and expansion plans, considering their long-term impact on the city's financial health. We prioritized projects that would generate a positive return on investment and have a sustainable impact on the community. In addition to exploring diversifying revenue sources to ensure sustainability of services and to manage risks. Investing in alternative funding sources somewhat mitigated the impact of state property tax policy HF 718 on general fund services. There are two major unattractive proposals on the table for council consideration. I am afraid we have no choice but to revisit and push for them. Time will tell.

Iowa Property Tax Reform

The legislators' stated goal is to incentivize local governments to make sound, long-term fiscal decisions, placing significant pressure on us. The state's objective has been to lower taxes. So, the state has been layering limitations on local governments with a considerable compounding effect. The HF718 bill, with its limitations on revenue growth and elimination of levying authority, claims to ensure Iowa's competitiveness as a state for business growth. I am concerned that it may be counterproductive, as it overlooks the potential impact on communities credit worthiness and quality of life—the primary driver for housing and job locations nowadays. This oversight could lead communities to deprioritize investing in quality of life and economic development efforts or live beyond their means, making it challenging to recruit both the workforce and employers. The bill has profound implications for local government leadership in small communities, placing us in a challenging position stuck between inflation and state policy limits. Worse yet, leadership ends up fleeing the profession as the job becomes impossible because of the burnout, leaving communities worse off. Both leadership flight and poor financial health have a serious long-term impact.

My strategy has been:

1. Advocate for local governments, educating and sharing current and potential long-term impacts. Leveraging relationships with community leaders to amplify messages. And engaging with all levels of stakeholders, including officials and economic development leaders.

2. Focus on storytelling.

3. Efficiency and effectiveness has always been our goal. That's what we do. We maximize.

4. Revisit the service delivery model. Have a bigger conversation with the community. Prioritize growth to leverage economies of scale.

5. Review the cost recovery model to ensure self-sustainability for enterprise operations. Revisit general fund expenditures, isolating those fundable through other levies and overhead allocations.

6. Explore alternative revenue sources to sustain service levels, emphasizing creativity. Be open to and encourage innovation and creativity.

7. Look for consolidation and partnerships for shared services, especially with the school district, neighboring jurisdictions, and county. Some services make more sense to coordinate and provide regionally.

8. Prioritize programs and services for optimal resource allocation.

9. Take care of staff. Why? because none of the above will happen without my awesome team.

Budget decisions may not always be well-received by those on the receiving end. However, I am confident in my decision-making process and dedicated to fulfilling my role. Working for the public interest, my responsibility is to recommend a sustainable budget that maximizes value, not necessarily to be liked. This is part of my leadership responsibility, to make tough decisions. I am aware that my intentions may be misunderstood and met with negativity because not everyone will understand and like my decisions, but I can rest easy at night with a clear conscience, knowing that I have done my due diligence and fulfilled my duties to the best of my ability.

Critical Infrastructure

One of the crucial aspects of my role is ensuring that the City's infrastructure is adequate, well-maintained, and serving the needs of the community. Baseline is the logical first step. I embarked on a comprehensive assessment of the city's social structure, roads, parks, utilities, and public facilities. With the help of my dedicated staff and expert consultants, we confirmed areas that required immediate attention. Armed with a strategy, developed criteria for prioritizing and a process for balancing short and long-term improvements. Striking a balance between various interests, competing needs, and priorities is a city manager's ongoing challenge. However, by taking a rational and transparent approach, you can make informed decisions that benefit the collective. Your goal is to help create a thriving city by making sustainable strategic decisions, engaging stakeholders, and mitigating negative consequences.

The City's infrastructure is the backbone that supports its growth and development. Like the intricate network of veins and arteries in the human body, it facilitates the smooth functioning of daily life, serving and connecting people, businesses, and resources. However, just as time weathers and erodes the sturdiest of structures, infrastructure requires regular evaluation and attention. We began by assessing the needs and condition of the roads, which are the lifelines connecting neighborhoods, businesses, and essential services and our wastewater processing capacity. My team and I evaluated our plans for new construction and reconstruction. Like the nervous system that enables communication and coordination within the body, reliable infrastructure systems are essential for the city's well-being.

Here I am face to face with a great challenge, a wastewater treatment plant improvement project and a deadline looming close by. The city is looking to grow and its processing capacity is maxed and under a compliance schedule for overloading and disinfectant requirements from the Iowa Department of Natural Resources due to standards. While road conditions or quality are easy to spot, despite its importance, the sewage system goes unnoticed. The wastewater utility plays a vital role in the city's daily functioning, providing an essential service and can limit growth if the facility lacks capacity. We reviewed proposed facility improvement plans specifically reviewed the new system's capacity to make sure improvements meet the evolving needs of the community. However, building a brand-new facility without an added capacity to at least accommodate its developable land, for a city aiming to grow its commercial and residential base is out of the question, but can be a costly endeavor. The challenges primarily arise from the city's financial capacity to support a large-scale (100 million) construction project during a time of inflation and hardship. We are determined to prevent overburdening our residents and committed to finding viable solutions. There you go, figure it out, city manager.

Increasing the wastewater treatment capacity is crucial to accommodate the anticipated growth and ensure the city can effectively handle the additional waste generated by new businesses and residents. However, the cost of such a project can be significant, encompassing infrastructure upgrades, technology, and construction expenses. Balancing the need for expansion with the financial constraints necessitates careful planning, analysis, and exploration of alternative funding sources. To mitigate the risk of burdening residents with excessive costs, we considered various strategies. The solution has to be a combination of reduced or phased-out improvements to spread burden over generations, revisiting cost allocation and rate structure, subsidizing rate with property taxes, seeking longer-term financing to spread cost burden across generations, and seeking grants and financial assistance from state or federal agencies to alleviate the financial strain on the city's budget.

Can you salvage a project in distress?

I joined the city at the tail of a long court battle and in the midst of a hot mess, sore feelings and flaming propaganda. How do you pick up and recover the shattered pieces? You try. Controversial projects do often fail if not rolled out with a proper communication strategy. It is vital to approach stakeholders with a friendly attitude and utmost respect to engage in the project idea and clearly convey the reasoning behind decisions, and the plan for addressing any adverse impacts. Remember people are emotional and sentimental and can be easily offended. Properties are a sensitive subject but proper communication ensures that stakeholders understand the considerations and trade-offs involved. By fostering open and direct communication, you build trust and maintain the support of the community.

Economic development projects are exceptionally challenging. In the absence of trust, those long-range planning goals are impossible to accomplish, especially when impacts are upfront. Take the regional airport project as an example. The city and its partners took on the project to proactively build for the future, focusing on improving the business environment to encourage its growth. The opportunity for receiving federal dollars to leverage local monies is a no brainer. The anticipated return on investment is expected to lower the cost of service eventually, addressing city concerns regarding service cost overburden on community residents. The 40 million dollar investment is expected to invite more investment in the community building on and key to a multimodal transportation plan but the project continues to face substantial delays because of opposition and emotional reactions. The rural community completely missed the point and purpose of the project and perceived it as an attack on their pride and an assault on their livelihood.

Rolling out the project without a tailored communication strategy created vulnerabilities and allowed opposition and opportunistic interests, often characterized as "sketch artists," to exploit critical aspects of the project. The opposition took advantage of the initial communication gap and was the first to present their case pushing a "David versus Goliath" narrative. In such situations, emotions tend to take precedence over reason, especially when conflict becomes a compelling narrative, which was further exacerbated by sensationalist media coverage.

This project serves as a clear example of falling victim to the "Not in My Backyard" (NIMBY) matrix (Credit Patric Slevin). The NIMBY phenomenon occurs when individuals vigorously oppose developments or projects that may affect their immediate surroundings, even if those projects have broader community benefits. It is an undertaking to counter narrative that has been digging roots in those unsuspecting minds for a decade and found itself meshed into folk tales. The city will continue to push for its future and full steam ahead. Truth will always prevail. I hope it is not too late for this community to realize that "it is not wise to rescue desperation". And it should invest in inspiration, instead. Rural Mahaska is a key stakeholder and is well represented in this community vision. This community will thrive or die together. There's no way around it.

To navigate such challenges successfully, it is crucial for leaders to have a comprehensive communication strategy in place from the outset. The strategy should not only convey the project's objectives and benefits but also carefully consider the approach with those potentially impacted and address potential concerns and engage the community in mitigation efforts. If we proactively involve stakeholders early in the process, it is possible to mitigate opposition and promote a more informed and rational discourse around the project's merits. Since we are talking about economic development, let's expand a little on my approach to economic development.

Economic Development Approach

Small communities are known to struggle with attracting businesses and workforce at a pace that supports economic growth. At the same time, in rural areas, leaders have a hard time pushing forward economic development plans because there's an alarming lack of understanding of the concept. This lack of understanding can make it difficult for leaders to garner support for the initiatives that could potentially bring growth and prosperity to those communities. My approach has been to focus on promoting economic development efforts, including branding and working closely with local partners to create a welcoming business environment. The goal is to highlight the interconnectedness, indirect impacts, and the city as a committed partner in helping create more opportunities and a sustainable economy, besides making sure we have adequate housing and infrastructure to support that growth.

Because the trajectory of the community is what we are mainly concerned about, economic development is a fundamental task and a key priority for the city manager. A vibrant economy would not only provide job opportunities for residents but also enhance the overall quality of life in the city. I was pleased when our strategic planning process confirmed thriving and a vibrant community as two of the four priority focus areas. Well, visioning is easy. The true test is in execution and community support of those visions. My team took a multifaceted approach that combined identifying our competitive advantage, building our brand, telling our story, investing in quality of life, marketing and recruiting efforts, investment in the built environment, and collaboration with our stakeholders. All those components intended to work in tandem to support our vision.

The strategic planning SWOT analysis (strengths, weaknesses, opportunities, and threats) highlighted the need for telling our story and the limited understanding of the indirect nature of economic development efforts. It was apparent that targeted marketing campaigns are needed to promote the city as a great place to be and an attractive destination for business. We identified the unique strengths, resources, and opportunities our town had to offer. The next step is to build a narrative that highlights our community's welcoming environment, rich history, great resources, advantage, and supportive community, portraying it as a place where businesses thrive and families enjoy living.

Focus on Quality of Life

Part of our strategic priorities is to focus on prioritizing investment in placemaking, promoting and increasing arts and culture opportunities to facilitate quality experience for residents, businesses, and visitors. The overarching strategy is to highlight, build on, and grow opportunities in the community. This is done through city investments in planning, physical improvements that support quality experience, city programming, partnerships that support quality of life efforts, and or facilitating support for those community assets in collaboration with community partners such as Oskaloosa Mainstreet, YMCA, MCRF and the Arts and Culture round table with our library being front and center to the conversation.

THRIVING COMMUNITY: QUALITY HOUSING & INFRASTRUCTURE AS ECONOMIC DEVELOPMENT TOOLS

Investing in housing has long been a top priority for our city. My approach emphasizes housing development as the most effective economic development strategy. By incentivizing and facilitating housing growth, we not only address the community's housing needs but also spark broader economic development. This investment creates jobs, improves infrastructure, revitalizes communities, and enhances the city's affordability and sustainability. For instance, population growth leads to economies of scale in city services, job creation, and stimulates economic activity, infrastructure development, and long-term economic resilience.

Infrastructure development is a crucial component of our economic development strategy. We continue to invest in improving transportation networks, ensuring adequate utilities, and enhancing the overall business environment. We recognized that infrastructure and housing quality are critical economic development tools to attract and retain businesses.

Marketing Opportunity & Incentives

To incentivize businesses to choose our town as their home, we highlighted our certified site, Main Street, and our development friendly environment, partnership opportunity, and the various business incentive programs we offer. Between Chambers and City, our typical incentives include grants, rebates, forgivable loans, and partnerships that we customize to attract new businesses and encourage the expansion of existing ones. These incentives are carefully designed to strike a balance between attracting and catalyzing investment and ensuring a fair return on the community's investment.

Facilitating Process

Collaboration with local organizations, Mahaska Chambers and development Group, school district, Mahaska Health Hospital, and William Penn university plays a vital role in our economic development efforts both as a driver for growth and as a business attraction. As a team, we continue to invest in community sustainability and partnerships to advance community priorities including recruiting and aligning workforce training programs with the needs of local businesses. By focusing on growing a skilled workforce, we enhance the city's appeal as a business-friendly community.

We continue to collaborate with Chambers and Greater Des Moines Partnership on creating a system for working closely with existing businesses, understanding their needs and challenges, and providing resources and support. The intent is to be responsive to business needs and to facilitate collaboration among businesses, encouraging and promoting the city's economic vitality. Our overarching strategy is to facilitate networking, knowledge sharing, and collaboration.

Building City Brand

We are focusing on building our brand through improvement efforts in terms of our decision making process, fiscal responsibility, and competitive advantage as a great place to be and a perfect partner. Telling our story and being both a welcoming community and a smart, healthy, and capable organization. We embody our values and are methodical with our planning and execution processes.

Utilizing the Opportunity in City Properties

Cities end up holding titles for a lot of properties for different reasons. It is advisable for a city to consider placing those properties back onto the tax roll and making them available for community use. These properties may include those acquired through right-of-way acquisition, condemnation, nuisance abatement, or for purposes that are no longer relevant. Placing those properties back on the tax roll and for community use can be a strategic move to increase tax base, generate revenue, stimulate development, and improve the overall quality of life for residents. Those properties can serve as an opportunity for partnership or an economic development incentive. Utilization should be done thoughtfully to ensure the best outcomes.

Placing properties back on the tax roll is a multifaceted strategy that fosters financial sustainability, community development, economic prosperity, and efficient resource management for cities. Unused or underutilized properties can be repurposed for community development initiatives. This might involve converting vacant lots into affordable housing or other facilities that benefit the community. Returning them to productive use can reduce the maintenance cost burden on city resources.

Economic development is a multifaceted effort aimed at attracting and retaining businesses. Through promoting the community and business incentives, collaboration with local stakeholders, and investing in infrastructure and housing development, we are intentional about creating a supportive business friendly environment. Our goal is to stimulate economic growth, create job opportunities, and foster a sustainable economy. We understood that a thriving local economy would not only enhance financial stability but also contribute to the overall well-being of our residents. It would provide them with employment options and support local services and amenities.

Feral Cats Colony: Do not You dare

Parks offer vital environmental, aesthetic, and recreational benefits to cities. They serve various purposes, shape city and neighborhood character, and act as tools for revitalization and economic development. Investing in parks is crucial for enhancing community health and well-being. Those facilities are like the community's living room. They foster social interaction and enrich the lives of the residents. As part of my initial assessment, checking the state of these facilities is a prerequisite for a robust capital improvement planning strategy, considering factors such as maintenance and the adequacy of amenities. The goal is to ensure that these spaces remain vibrant and inviting, catering to the diverse needs and interests of the community. Through the learning process, staff shared concerns regarding the unsanitary condition of a park shelter at the main historical park. The shelter was taken over by a feral-cat colony that apparently called the park home. Suggesting relocation unleashed a tide of emotions surrounding the colony and a real confrontation with the cats' feeders. The park cleanup discussion had the most turnout and was the most well attended council meeting since I started.

The room was packed and spilling over. I can feel the eyes piercing through my skin. The new city manager is a cat hater. And I can't help but find irony in the situation. My mind immediately goes to the hilarious cat story from my time on the City of Marion team, courtesy of Chief Kitsmiller, a fantastic storyteller. I remember when he shared a hilarious cat story that had me laughing uncontrollably—tears streaming down my face. Little did I know that moment would continue to brighten my days. Upon arriving at my office in Oskaloosa, I found a package from Kitsmiller sitting on my desk. My assistant told me it came from Marion. I started laughing and told her it was a cat because I was certain that it was going to be. Inside was a framed team picture with everyone holding a cat. Never fails. Every time I look at it, a smile forms on my face. Even thinking about it right now takes me back to that memorable story and makes me miss my people. Long story short, cats are now associated with joy.

Anyway, "Compromise" was the word of the day. It is ok to figure out a process and path forward together. But the park quality was nonnegotiable. Responsibility and accountability through a contract and a relocation process are a must to hold the city harmless. Some people may never understand those decisions and we will have to live with that.

Armed with the findings from assessments, we developed a comprehensive strategy for infrastructure improvements including revitalizing, funding, and outlining the necessary steps and investments required to address existing deficiencies and prepare for future growth. We prioritized projects based on urgency, impact, and available resources, ensuring a strategic and efficient approach. As we follow these plans, we highlighted the need for incorporating systems planning with comprehensive planning and the ongoing monitoring and maintenance schedule. Accountability favors specificity and needs to be at the forefront. What is the life cycle cost? Who is responsible? And who is accountable? Who needs to be informed? By adopting a proactive approach, we aimed to minimize disruptions, enhance safety, and maximize the lifespan of those assets.

We partnered with the Mahaska County Conservation Commission and the Iowa State University's Community Design Lab to develop a comprehensive park system plan with a complete inventory and assessment of recreational opportunities and facilities. The scope includes documenting and visualizing existing conditions, concerns and opportunities for parks and trail systems in Mahaska County. The documentation was meant to aid in developing design strategies for future park enhancements and open space development. The plan is designed to promote our community and includes vision, strategy, and marketing tools to promote the amenities and the opportunity in them as an economic driver.

Assessing infrastructure was a crucial phase. Our collaborative and proactive approach to community development is also key. It was critical to conduct comprehensive evaluations, identifying areas in need of attention and developing plans for improvement. By addressing current issues and planning for the future, we ensure that the city remains vibrant, safe, and prepared for future growth. Through careful strategic planning for maintenance and investments, we aim to preserve the city's infrastructure as the foundation for the community's prosperity and well-being.

Review Existing Deals

Governments often face challenges in terms of agility and adaptability. The size and complexity of government organizations can make it challenging to respond swiftly to changing circumstances. It is wise to regularly reassess positions and policies because the conditions and needs are constantly evolving. I will not delve into specifics here, but I would like to emphasize the value of cultivating a habit of reviewing and adapting to changing circumstances. In certain situations, cities may find it necessary to disentangle themselves from unfavorable or disadvantageous agreements. It is worth noting that each situation is unique, and the specific steps and strategies for getting out of an unfavorable or a bad deal will depend on the nature of the agreement and the applicable contractual frameworks. Seeking professional advice and carefully considering the implications of each approach is crucial in achieving the most favorable outcome for the city.

Cities may have agreements in place that no longer serve their best interests due to changing economic, environmental, or social factors. For instance, economic downturns might make certain financial commitments unsustainable. After thorough evaluations, the next crucial step is to act. In some cases, the situation may require making tough, even unpopular decisions. The ability to make tough decisions is an inherent and essential aspect of effective leadership. Such decisions often involve intricate factors, conflicting interests, and the possibility of trade-offs. Leaders must carefully navigate these complexities to make the best possible choices and enhance the likelihood of achieving optimal outcomes.

In complex decision-making scenarios, leaders may encounter conflicting interests. It is crucial for them to carefully weigh these competing priorities and make choices that align with the city's overarching values and objectives. It is important to assess the potential consequences of each available option. I default to evaluating both the immediate and long-term impact of decisions on different stakeholders, including individuals, organizations, and society at large. Balancing diverse perspectives and engaging in a collaborative problem-solving process can facilitate a more inclusive decision-making approach and help mitigate potential conflicts. But the bottom line should always serve the public interest, necessitating a full understanding of the potential risks, benefits, and implications associated with each course of action.

As a leader you must be able to live with the fact that making tough decisions is not about seeking popularity but about acting in the best interest of your team, organization, or the greater community you serve. Such decisions may involve restructuring, budget cuts, firing, personnel changes, or other actions that can be emotionally charged and require a strong resolve.

Effective leaders approach these tough decisions with a combination of empathy, fairness, and a clear understanding of their objectives and values. Being strong enough to make hard decisions is what separates leaders from others. You be true to your values and clear about your decision-making process and be courageous enough to live with being disliked. Leaders consider the long-term benefits and consequences of their choices. They effectively communicate the "why" reconsideration was necessary. While these decisions can be tough, they are often necessary to drive progress, navigate challenges, and lead organizations toward their goals.

There are strategies you can utilize to enhance your ability to lead objectively and efficiently, minimizing the influence of emotions and political considerations on your business decisions. Consider committing to the following:

1. Data-Driven Decision-Making:

   Base decisions on data and evidence rather than emotions or political considerations. Utilize factual information to support your choices.

2. Establish Clear Criteria:

   Define clear criteria and benchmarks for decision-making. This helps in maintaining objectivity and ensures that decisions align with predetermined standards.

3. Remind everyone to focus on goals, eyes on the prize:

   Keep the organization's mission and goals at the forefront of decision-making. This provides a framework that guides decisions toward the overall objectives.

4. Review and Reflect:

   Regularly review decisions and their outcomes. Reflect on whether they align with organizational goals and whether any adjustments are needed.

Key Takeaways

Cities need to periodically review and adjust their positions and agreements as conditions change. This flexibility and responsiveness are essential for effective governance and ensuring that cities can adapt to evolving circumstances in the best interest of their residents.

"Life is filled with difficult decisions, and winners are those who make them" Dan Brown. Making tough decisions is an inherent part of leadership. Leaders embrace the challenge, leaning on their analytical skills and courage to navigate tough choices. They must be prepared to tackle challenging choices, guided by their vision, values, and a commitment to doing what is best for their team, organization, and community, even when those choices are difficult or unpopular.

Leaders understand that their choices can have wide-ranging impacts and must be willing to shoulder the weight of those decisions. Making tough decisions requires courage. Leaders must have the conviction to stand by their choices, even in the face of criticism or opposition. They must be willing to make tough calls, even if they are unpopular, to advance the greater good. They stick to ethical principles and their organization's values when making tough decisions. They consider the impact on stakeholders, weigh considerations, and ensure that their choices align with the organization's mission and vision. They carefully analyze information, evaluate potential risks and benefits, and consider the short-term and long-term implications of decisions. They seek input from relevant stakeholders, consult subject matter experts, and conduct thorough research to make informed choices.

> "Courage is what it takes to stand up and speak; courage is also what it takes to sit down and listen."
>
> - Winston Churchill.

Leaders remain open to learning from both successes and failures, adjusting their approach as needed. They communicate their decisions clearly, explaining their reasoning and the factors considered. They must strive to be transparent and open, helping others understand the context and rationale for the tough choices made.

CHAPTER 9

MAINTAINING TRAJECTORY: DISCIPLINE & COMMITMENT

"What you spend years building may be destroyed overnight. Build it anyway."

— Mother Teresa

The community thrives when both its leadership and stakeholders are engaged and equally invested in its development. The city manager cannot help a community that is not willing to be involved in helping itself. And without a plan or a system to guard against social pressure and decision fatigue, we tend to drift, resulting in less favorable outcomes and no satisfaction in the work we do. In this chapter, I will discuss the tenets of my strategy for operationalizing our vision in a way that helps with maintaining a successful trajectory. From strategic plan development and implementation to coffee talks, I sought to create platforms for open dialogue and collaboration to facilitate alignment and to grow together in the pursuit of our shared vision.

Approach to Strategic Planning

"There is no power for change greater than a community discovering what it cares about."

Margaret J. Wheatley

The approach I took to strategic planning was a unique one, taking a community approach rather than an organizational approach. I invited community stakeholders including school district, county, university, non-profit leaders, business leaders, and the local hospital with a goal of putting together a plan that all can relate to. We all contribute to the vitality of our community, each of us playing a distinct role, and are actively working on improving conditions. As integral members, we collectively share the responsibility of cultivating an environment that nurtures growth and prosperity. The proposed process was meant to be a robust way to organize our efforts, defining and focusing on priorities and to hold each other accountable for our part. For example, if the goal is to grow the community by recruiting workforce and families, it doesn't matter how well the city does in terms of level of service and availability of housing, if the school quality is not up to bar or if the healthcare services are not available or don't meet expectations.

We started with a session where stakeholders came together to share their concerns and voice their opinions. We first conducted "Strengths, Weaknesses, Opportunities, Threats (SWOT) analysis with city and county staff members. Why? because those are the boots on the ground who know more about our limitations. And then followed by a group session with community partners, then a work session with elected officials, Council and County Supervisors. Additional feedback was gathered through two listening sessions before the 2024-2026 plan was put together. The plan constituted our north star as a community and included four focus areas, underlying strategies, and values to orient and guide efforts well into the future. Sessions were facilitated by the newly appointed city manager and School Superintendent served as bonding exercises. Timing couldn't have been better and I couldn't have picked a better partner. They were in the form of open dialogue, actively listening to the ideas and perspectives put forth by attendees. These meetings allowed us to focus efforts on addressing pressing issues, to gather feedback on proposed projects, and to ensure that partners are included in decision-making processes. By adopting a collaborative process, we fostered ownership, empowerment, and accountability.

Execution System: Operationalizing The Vision

"Success is the sum of small efforts, repeated day in and day out."

- Robert Collier

In the public sector success equates to resilience and requires acknowledging the potential for small changes and the impact of ripple effects. Consistent effort is key to making change and improvement stick. No matter how hard, I continue to emphasize the importance of staying committed to our goals and working toward them. The establishment of a robust system plays a pivotal role in shaping habits and behaviors that are invaluable to maintaining performance rhythms, even during challenging and imperfect times.

My approach to executing the strategic plan involves the development of an annual work plan process, effectively translating the overarching vision into operational incremental tasks. This process accounts for all activity and ties performance to goals and objectives and ensures a clear line of sight from strategic objectives to day-to-day activities. Everyone on the team should know the vision inside and out and how day to day business and behavior advance the goals. Simply, we ought to embody who we want to be and commit to habits guided by the overarching implementation strategy.

The annual work plan is a planning and prioritization system that outlines specific tasks and objectives that align with the broader vision, ensuring that the organization's efforts are directed towards achieving its long-term goals. The emphasis lies on meticulous tracking, accountability, and facilitating a seamless integration of long-term goals into the fabric of daily tasks.

The team should be engaged in conversations about the metrics, how we know if we are successful and give input into defining success. Get in the habit of meeting with the team regularly to review progress toward goals. Your strategy is just a theory, and your plan is your best-informed guess of what gets you to succeed. So, make sure they are living documents. Adjust as you go based on the available information and adapt to team needs. The system will make big tasks seem easy. The team will surprise you with "out-performing" your plans if you succeed as their lead. When metrics are hard to define, it is even more critical to clarify and over communicate vision, goals, and objectives. If the team cannot articulate the connection between their daily activities and the strategic plan, implementing and achieving goals becomes challenging. It's crucial that the team is able to justify their actions and is trained to link small tactics back to the vision by consistently asking fundamental questions: Why is it a good idea? Why? and Why? The third "Why" is the answer you are looking for. This process helps uncover the root causes and ensures a clear alignment with the overarching strategic plan.

Collaboration with community organizations is a great avenue for engagement. These organizations are the lifeblood of the city, dedicated to serving the needs and interests of the community. By forging partnerships, as a community, we tap into expertise, resources, and grassroot networks, amplifying our collective impact. Together, we share the responsibility of creating an environment for growth.

Annual reports that align partners' accomplishments and planning efforts with that of the organization are synced as part of the budget process. Close partners such as Chambers, Mainstreet, and Animal Shelter reflect on the previous year to better position the team for the following year.

Community revitalization projects are of higher priority. My team supported and collaborated with interested local groups to enhance the aesthetics of the city parks, create inviting gathering places, and celebrate community uniqueness. By involving the community and letting initiatives such as dancing lights and painting with lights drive transformational endeavors, we invite a sense of ownership and shared responsibility for beauty and vitality.

Broader Community Engagement

Engaging the community was at the core of my learning process and is a basic tenet of my execution strategy. I recognized that the collective wisdom and participation of stakeholders are essential in shaping the city's identity and driving its progress. I was aiming to harmonize the voices of the community, creating a symphony of ideas and solutions. We may start with tolerance and a room for differences allowing urban and rural to contribute. Engagement requires intent and willingness to learn and unlearn. I fully believe that understanding is a process. I was successful at times and failed sometimes. And that is ok. Promoting positivity, open dialogue, constructive communication, and inclusivity can help create a supportive community environment. Just like individual relationships, community relationship building is a long commitment to building trust and maintaining respect and striving for alignment.

> *"If you want to go quickly, go alone. If you want to go far, go together."*
>
> – African Proverb

As part of community engagement, we invited a group of young professionals from diverse backgrounds who are interested in addressing community needs and in serving as change agents and advocates for the big picture. We solicited ideas and used the group as a conduit to connect with young Oskaloosa. They gave a lot of insights into communication needs and appreciated the open dialogue with the City Manager.

Through input meetings and collaboration with community and organizations, we created avenues for open dialogue and collaboration. By supporting community efforts, we built a solid foundation for residents to actively participate in shaping the city's future. Together, we embarked on a journey of growth towards a vibrant, inclusive, and thriving community, driven by the collective power of its engaged people. And by nurturing a culture of optimism, ownership, and respect, we can thrive, attract investment, and effectively address challenges for the betterment of all residents. We have got to figure out how we row together in the same direction.

Normalizing Review

After action review and respectful constructive feedback should be normalized. Leaders create the conditions for it and are responsible for sustaining those conditions. The Leader should be critical of learning and progress and communicate vision and goals. That is what you do every day. Your eyes are on the prize. The Team should understand the goal is to improve. Follow up, check-in, reflect, and learn to pivot to be ahead of the curve. Success will take not only staying committed but also learning how to learn and improve. Let constructive feedback and reflection be the norm. Celebrate successes and failures. It is about learning, building, and improving. And always remember the difference between battle and war. It is ok to lose a battle, your eye is on winning the war. We are creatures of habit. The habit will cause the team to naturally engage in critical thinking about what went well and what could be improved when reporting on progress and reflecting on actions taken. Positive reinforcement is proven to be far more effective than other strategies.

As I concentrate on propelling team performance forward, I do not demand perfection from people. Instead, I prioritize maintaining momentum because imperfections are inevitable. We are human, prone to mistakes and negative thoughts. Simply put, plans do not always unfold seamlessly. I celebrate our trajectory and momentum, nurture confidence, and help in learning how to navigate emotions and swiftly recover when we encounter obstacles. I do, however, insist on a commitment to respect, kindness, and continuous improvement or growth. You do not get fit in a day. You get fit only when you commit to your exercise routine. You know it is a gradual process and it depends on your attitude and level of commitment. I will hold my team accountable for their commitment and I reward the "try" and celebrate courage. Having hard conversations is part of the growth process and it is how we can be authentic and honest. "If you're afraid to offend, you can't be honest." Thomas Pane. We must be able to address issues head on with courage, kindness, and utmost integrity. There is so much kindness in the truth.

Our world is constantly evolving, and our ability to adapt is what keeps us relevant and successful. I urge our team to embrace flexibility, welcome innovative ideas and remain poised to pivot. Let us be open to adjusting our strategies, even our opinions, to ensure they align with the evolving needs of our organization and stakeholders. Sebastian Enges puts it together nicely when he talks about growth. "If you are growing, you're constantly going to be updating your opinion. I reserve the right to at any time update my opinion of something. Because I fully understand I can speak from the truth which I consciously am at. But, if I continually grow from my level of consciousness, my perception is going to change." Change in perception sort of is evidence of growth, intelligence, and open mindedness. When you are growing, your perception of things changes.

Reporting Out: Storytelling

There's a sacrificial aspect to public service, driven by community and a pursuit of fulfillment. If we fail to effectively tell our story and communicate our narrative and "until lions learn how to write, every story will glorify the hunter (Achebe)

Budgets and Work Plans are execution plans. Communicating the rationale and outcomes of these plans should be integrated into both the planning and budgeting processes. There's tremendous value in reporting back to the community the value added in keeping both staff and the community engaged and involved with the improvement process. Sharing updates on progress, raising awareness about issues and roadblocks, and highlighting accomplishments fosters more engagement, builds optimism and confidence in the process and in the leadership.

Administrators and leadership teams should learn how to effectively tell the story of public sector initiatives. Public sector budgeting is challenging due to the potential for narratives that may run counter to community interests. Effective communication is crucial to ensure alignment with the community's needs and priorities. It seems that some state legislators[2] hold a dangerous mindset viewing local governments as wasteful and unaccountable that they felt the need to tighten rules a bit to tame. "Des Moines Register poll reported 58 percent of Iowans supported "initiatives to 'cut property taxes, limiting what local governments could spend on services.'" Needless to say, local governments are not in the business of making money. We run very lean, mostly supported by volunteerism and community contribution, to provide vital services for our communities. We are inefficient, yes. Just like all governments, because of the inherent nature of bureaucracy and dictated process, not because we are wasteful! The perfect example for this is Chapter26 that we are having to deal with and being blamed for its impact at the same time. I understand that policies sometimes have unintended consequences but adopting a frugal policy is not necessarily a wise approach. The system is being abused and communities are paying the cost. So many tax dollars are being wasted on legal services because of the lowest bid idea. Our fear of corruption is crippling us.

Regular budget performance monitoring and reporting are essential for management decisions and to ensure team accountability. We closely tracked both our strategic plan and budget performance. This allows us to make informed adjustments, identify potential areas for improvement, and ensure that resources are allocated efficiently and effectively. Our budget process is a cycle that starts with strategic planning and ends with reporting on the strategic planning outcomes. I believe

---

[2] https://www.clintonherald.com/opinion/a-look-at-iowa-s-new-property-tax-relief-bill-house-file-718/article_3f0d67d8-84f4-11ee-9cb6-cbc2a6a04c50.html

this way we are committed to constantly learning, evaluating, adapting, and holding ourselves accountable. We need to learn how to come up with user-friendly formats and build storytelling in the process to bring other people along with us, especially the community and our legislators. I know you are thinking we don't have the resources. But, I would say treat it as top priority and carve out the resources for it because after HF718, this now proven can make or break us. Make it a priority and train your team to excel at it.

Key Takeaway

If you don't know how to tell a story, you don't have a way to persuade people.

Understanding Enemies of Progress

"Know the enemy and know yourself in a hundred battles you will never be in peril"

Sun Tzu (DeSutter, Paula A).

"You may not control all the events that happen to you, but you can decide not to be reduced by them"

Maya Angelo

Communities face numerous challenges that require collective effort to address and overcome for a better tomorrow. Many of these challenges are unique to the public service sector, constituting the problems that city leadership grapples with, and most of the time hindering or slowing down progress. Depending on the severity of those issues, if the community is not onboard, they may render the city manager's efforts useless, just like a one hand trying to clap. It is important for communities to be aware of these challenges, as they may be standing between them and realizing their vision. As well, emerging leaders should have full understanding of these issues and knowledge about potential obstacles or threats as it is crucial for effective decision-making.

Resources Constraints:

It is common for organizations to face resource constraints. Creative solutions are helpful such as revisiting the service delivery model, seeking partnerships for shared services with other organizations, pursuing grants, and seeking alternative funding sources. But the most fundamental and effective strategy is optimizing existing resources through efficient allocation and prioritization.

Economic constraints: limitations impacting the implementation of initiatives.

Long-range Strategy:

1. Look for innovative ways to leverage existing resources and explore public-public and public-private partnerships.

2. Utilize economic development tools to fund public infrastructure.

3. Efficient and effective allocation of resources

4. Grow. Pursue economic development opportunities, attract investments, and support local businesses to boost economic growth.

5. Prioritize investment in infrastructure: Outdated infrastructure and limited access to technology will hinder progress. *Strategy:*

1. Prioritize technology infrastructure upgrades and collaborate with relevant stakeholders to bridge these gaps.

2. Adopt digital transformation initiatives to improve efficiency, service delivery, and overall city administration.

3. Prioritize investment in infrastructure to encourage and guide growth.

Lack of Trust:

Lack of public trust is the most concerning issues facing city organizations and threatening leadership effectiveness nowadays. Research indicates that trust in government is dwindling and has become a serious issue to the level of impeding policy, budgeting, and strategic planning. According to a leadership survey, 58 percent of respondents ranked "lack of trust" as the top challenge. Overall, trust emerged as a more significant challenge compared to funding issues (46 percent) and budgeting issues (42 percent), which are typically viewed as primary challenges confronting local governments today. (Church, 2024).

Insight: Building public trust and positive perception requires consistent and effective communication and delivery of results. It requires leadership and representation in the full sense of the word. Focus on proactive and positive communication, provide regular updates on progress, highlight positives, and celebrate achievements to enhance public confidence in the process. Have the courage to make tough decisions. In public service, reputation is utterly our most valuable quality. People trust you if they know your thought process and can predict your reactions. That knowledge represents the promise of a productive interaction and implies trustworthiness, reliability, and capability of delivering on your commitments. People are more likely to collaborate and form positive relationships when they have confidence in your organization. Maintaining a good reputation requires consistency. Act with integrity, demonstrate competence, and always treat others with respect and fairness. By consistently delivering on promises, being transparent and positive, we enhance our reputation and gain trust. To maintain your success trajectory, watchout for the following list, presence of any of them can seriously impact community progress. They say being aware of and acknowledging what's wrong is half of the solution.

Distorted Perspectives

Misunderstandings can occur when individuals misinterpret or misrepresent the intentions or implications of a proposed decision or policy. It can stem from either lack of knowledge, bias, or the tendency to jump to conclusions without thoroughly considering the facts. Negative mindset and ignorance about certain aspects of a policy or its underlying issues can lead to incomplete or completely distorted perspectives. As a result, reactions may sometimes be negative, disruptive, and childish, when individuals resort to personal attacks, insults, or bullying tactics instead of engaging in respectful and substantive discourse. Such behavior hinders productive dialogue, discourages open participation, and creates a toxic atmosphere that stifles progress.

"I've been all over the world and I've never seen a statue of a critic."

Leonard Bernstein

Have you ever seen a statue of a critic? No, because they are not builders. While I appreciate constructive criticism, the one that comes with a negative mindset can be toxic. Negative attitude and constant criticism simply discourage participation and divert energy away from the real issues and the constructive problem-solving efforts. The most detrimental impact is that they create divisions and conflicts, further impeding cooperation. Anyone paying attention to those stage hogs and keyboard warriors will know what I mean. Anyway, it is safe to say, if nothing can be learned from the criticism, it is just going to be hurtful and completely unnecessary.

In a community context, the problem is, people with a negative mindset or those emotionally immature like teenagers, are their own worst enemy. They are short sighted and so blinded by their ignorance and hatefulness that they are willing to stand in the way of progress at all costs, shooting themselves in the foot. They are less likely to seek common ground, find constructive solutions, or work towards goals. They only want to critique and complain. Such a mindset is wasteful, impedes growth, and prevents organizations from addressing the pressing issues effectively. Their behaviors or may I call them tantrums are very discouraging to members who want to participate or support community initiatives. Why? simply because rational people don't want to wrestle with a pig. When individuals are constantly exposed to negative attitudes, skepticism, and those swings of character assassination shots, they will be reluctant to take risks or contribute, limiting the community's potential for growth and advancement.

Negative Press: The Mother of Them All

The impact of negative press is compounded and can be far-reaching as the media plays a significant role in shaping public opinion and influencing the narrative around community initiatives and events. Negative media coverage can severely impact a community's success by distorting its image and eroding public trust, hindering economic development and creating divisions. When conflict is sensationalized, it overshadows all positive aspects, creating a negative perception among stakeholders and potential investors, ultimately leading to reduced confidence and therefore limited opportunity for growth.

No doubt that press as a business thrives when there's conflict and controversy because the two generate attention and tend to attract more viewership or readership. But, the negative coverage overtime can be especially damaging, holding the community back, counteracting its economic development efforts. When the focus on negatives overshadows the positives, it creates a skewed narrative that doesn't reflect reality accurately, inflating negatives. Exploiting conflict for personal gain takes this damage to another level, basically constructing a distorted image of the community, eroding public trust, and perpetuating a cycle of disadvantage. Why is this a big deal? Because the community's reputation impacts investment in both physical and social capital, and efforts to attract talent and to foster a sense of pride among residents. The distorted image of the community is created because of focusing on problems, conflicts, or shortcomings rather than on the community's strengths and potential. Just like those negative thoughts in your head, if you let them fester, they can lead you to depression and a complete devastation. Such depiction of the community deters people and businesses from establishing or expanding in the area, as people may perceive it as unfavorable or unstable. We all know that people vote with their feet. Potential investors may be hesitant to come to a community that is portrayed negatively, leading to a lack of investment. It also discourages skilled workforce from relocating to the area and therefore can further impede growth and development efforts.

Impact on Support: Negative coverage can discourage individuals and organizations from offering support, funding, or resources to community initiatives, especially those high-profile projects. Potential stakeholders may be hesitant to associate themselves with a community or a project that is highly controversial or portrayed negatively, leading to reduced opportunities for success.

Impact on Morale: Negative news is just disappointing and can very much dampen community morale, causing a decline in motivation, engagement, and participation. When community members constantly hear negative stories or criticisms, they may become disheartened, leading to decreased enthusiasm and limited effort towards achieving those important community goals. This typically manifests itself in low participation levels on public service boards and commissions and lack of engagement for projects.

Impact on Collaboration: Negative news exacerbates existing divisions within the community and creates new conflicts by misleading propaganda. Biased reporting is especially dangerous as it can polarize opinions, fragment the community, and impede the cooperation necessary for achieving critical objectives. The community ends up spending resources fighting its own demons, constituting a significant opportunity cost and a huge cause for setbacks.

Insight: Not sure what to tell you here other than focusing on communication and encouraging a culture of learning, ownership, and civic participation. You can focus on making efforts to bridge the gap between those individual goals and community development goals, highlighting the big picture. City managers are preachers. They plant seeds as they go hoping they will take root.

Individualistic Culture

When individuals primarily focus on their own advancement without considering the broader community interest, they create a fragmented society where the common good is neglected or overshadowed. The pursuit of one's own interests can very much exploit or be at odds with the community's interest. And the diminished sense of responsibility can limit opportunities for collaboration and the pooling of skills and resources needed for community growth and success.

Insight: Encourage a more communal mindset and promote leadership and a sense of social responsibility to help expose and counteract the negative impacts of excessive individualism. Raising awareness about the big picture and reinforcing the fact that the well-being of individuals is interconnected with the well-being of the community may help shift the mindset. Condemning or shaming selfish behavior and highlighting the values of cooperation and the importance of contributing to the greater good, may help with developing a broader understanding of their role within the community.

Complacency: "The price good men pay for indifference to public affairs is to be ruled by evil men" Plato. Complacency can be a significant barrier that holds a community back from making progress and reaching its full potential. Complacency arises when people are reluctant to step out of their comfort zones to take the reins, stick their neck out for what is right, or voice their opinion, fearing judgment or being shot down or simply as a result of diffusion of responsibility when they feel someone else would. They see setbacks and rejection as failures. It can manifest as a lack of social responsibility or a failure to support or recognize the need for defending improvement initiatives. Skipping votes on elections and dodging calls for civic duties are great examples of this irresponsible complacent behavior. They are responsible for the failure of important initiatives for their lack of participation and allowing the loud few to decide the fate of the community. Neutrality only helps the offensive party. You will find those in every community but the percentage will make a difference in its impact. If wide spread, a complacent mindset prevents the community from adapting and taking advantage of those opportunities for success.

Insight: Overcoming complacency requires collective effort. We only fail when we are unwilling to get up and try again. Community leaders play a crucial role in combating complacency by inspiring and mobilizing individuals towards action. They can foster a sense of urgency and communicate the benefits of change and improvement, engaging, educating, promoting active participation, and empowering individuals in our circles can help break the cycle of complacency.

Shortsightedness

Kicking the can down the road is an ugly common practice, when it comes to public infrastructure. Delaying action is convenient but lacks foresight and is somewhat irresponsible. This is the rich grounds for politics because it is impactful and it is easier to defer the cost rather than deal with an up roar. While fiscal responsibility is important, an excessive focus on cost-cutting and instant gratification in the short-term and the reluctance to invest in the future can have a detrimental effect on the community and its growth. Simply, deferred maintenance costs you more than addressing problems promptly and proactively. From a business perspective, this is a short-sighted approach that undermines long-term success. Cutting corners on essential resources and infrastructure to save a couple of bucks can compromise the whole community vision and its competitiveness. A community that fails to invest adequately in its development may face great challenges in attracting new businesses, retaining talent, and fostering economic growth. Downplaying and underestimating the impact of lack of support for those critical economic development initiatives is failure. Neglecting investments in critical infrastructure can also limit its ability to provide a high quality of life for its residents. Yes, it is important to be mindful of expenses and make wise financial decisions, but it is equally important to recognize the value of investing in the community's future, supporting initiatives that sustain the community's well-being in the long run. A smart approach that considers both financial health and strategic investments can yield long-term community benefits. This can be done through allocating resources wisely and investing in the community's growth, creating a business environment that contributes to a thriving economy, attracts more opportunities for development such as tax base, and provides a sustainable and better quality of life for residents.

Manipulators & Stage Hogs Combo

Watch out for the opportunistic few who choose to misrepresent the truth for personal gains, intentionally feeding ignorance as a tactic to mobilize, creating conflict and causing divisions. They tend to be aggressive and abusive. They use fear as a tool to intimidate others and go after people through cheap innuendo, gossip, and reputation destruction or straight out bullying. It is important to address misinformation publicly to ensure accuracy. Through focusing on providing accurate information and being open to engaging in constructive dialogue, you can effectively work towards a more informed and productive discourse around city decisions and projects.

Into the bargain, recognizing and addressing those manipulative forces that lurk in the dark is essential for maintaining a healthy community and for making progress on the community development agenda. Manipulative forces manifest themselves in various contexts, such as relationships, politics, and social dynamics. You can easily spot manipulators driven by self-interest as they often aim to gain an unfair advantage. Well, buckle up, if you happen to be among the few with a spine.

Insight: It's important to ensure that policy decisions are based on thoughtful analysis and inclusive dialogue rather than driven by the manipulative or those seeking to be in the spotlight. Unhealthy power dynamics erode trust. Stage hogs detract from substantive discussions, eroding trust, exacerbating polarization, and undermining your collaboration efforts. Be bold, show strength, build confidence in your leadership team, and invite more people along. When you encounter those who intentionally misrepresent the truth, show bias, and use ignorance as a tactic to mobilize opposition towards city decisions, it is crucial that you approach the situation with patience and the following strategy:

> **Maintain composure and professionalism:** It is important to stay composed and professional when engaging with individuals who intentionally misrepresent the truth. Stay focused on the facts, remain calm, and respond with reasoned arguments. Separate your emotions from the situation. It is not about you.

> **Be Empathetic:** try to understand the underlying motivations and concerns that drive these individuals to misrepresent the truth or exhibit bias. Practice empathy and listen attentively to their viewpoints, even when you strongly disagree. Empathy can help create a more conducive environment for finding common ground.

Engage in constructive dialogue: offer clear explanations of city decisions, policies, and actions, including context to help them understand the reasoning behind these decisions. Communicate the benefits and potential positive impacts on the community. While some people may exhibit an adversarial attitude, try to engage in constructive dialogue if possible. Simply counter misinformation with verifiable facts and evidence, presenting information in a respectful manner and providing accurate information to debunk false claims. Seek common ground to establish a foundation for productive conversation maintaining a focus on the city's best interests. I would watchout for cognitive bias. In that case, arguments are useless. Don't waste your time. You don't argue with a teenager.

Build Lily Pads

In the grand scheme of things, "Giving up is the only sure way to fail."

- Gena Showalter

All of these enemies of progress, we just talked about, create divisions, slowing you down and like a current beneath the surface undermining all your efforts. Now what? Generally speaking, you could build lily pads with sanity and reason in order to move the organization and community forward. I borrowed this term from President Obama when he was addressing the east-wing west-wing dissent and trying to create a foundation that is grounded in logical thinking and rational decision-making. My advice is, seek common ground and "if you can't be a bridge, be a lighthouse." Jefferson Fisher. The following are the principles I have incorporated into the leadership approach to help guide our decision-making process, promote effectiveness, and most importantly ensure that the team's actions reflect well on the city and align with the best interests of the community.

Critical thinking and Open-mindedness: Encourage the team to think critically and objectively. And promote a culture where ideas and proposals are evaluated based on their merits and supported by evidence and logical reasoning, rather than where those ideas came from. They should listen actively and respectfully to others' ideas and create opportunities for constructive debates and discussions.

Data-driven decision-making: Only base decisions on reliable data and information to minimize bias and make informed decisions that align with the goals of the city and interest of the community. Be methodical and be consistent about following the process. You have to follow the process. It's the only thing that is assuring.

Constructive problem-solving: encourage your team to approach challenges with a logical and methodical approach starting with Kidlin's law: "If you write the problem down clearly, then the matter is half solved". And identifying the root cause of the problem. Boy, when you write it down, you'll have a good perspective, as if you separate yourself from it. While maintaining a rational approach, acknowledge that emotions can influence decision-making. Encourage the team to get in the habit of considering the broader implications of their decisions.

Effective Communication: Encourage everyone to express their thoughts and ideas and emphasize active listening and sharing. Communication is key to minimizing misunderstandings and promoting rational discussions. Communication is effective when we adapt our messaging, approach, and attitude to our audience needs. Well, you have to know your audience first.

Ethical Conduct: This one is non-negotiable and goes without saying but it is important to remind everyone, in order to emphasize clarity. Adopt a culture of integrity, honesty, and accountability, ensuring that the leadership operates with reason and a high ethical conduct. "We will do the right thing, always, and regardless of how we feel"

CONCLUSION

My first two years as City Manager of this small city have been a period of significance and growth. Stepping up through team building, organizational development, system improvements, and economic development, I believe we have laid the groundwork for a vibrant future.

"Stepping Up" approach emphasizes the need for leaders to be intentional about orchestrating the alignment of their strategy, structure, and people to drive success. It underscores the importance of adaptability and the profound impact of leadership on team growth and organizational success. By leading with a growth mindset, leaders can elevate performance and can better navigate the complexities of city management, ultimately achieving both excellence and fulfillment in their roles.

As I look back on those years, I am filled with pride and gratitude for what my team has accomplished. The challenges we are facing are significant, but through perseverance and collaboration, we are able to hit our benchmarks. My greatest pride lies in the people and in building those meaningful connections. Our biggest accomplishment is establishing a solid foundation, streamlining our process, operationalizing the vision, and striving to maintain alignment. Strategic planning quarterly and annual reports will numerate and celebrate our achievements. We are conscious about the little things, the tactics, and the small steps that get us closer to achieving our vision every day. Seeing who we want to become and aligning our behaviors behind it is a big deal.

One of our major accomplishments as a team was organizing our infrastructure and growth plans, including establishing our decision-making process, criteria for evaluation, communication system, and platforms for reporting out and for engagement. Through careful planning we made progress towards addressing long-standing issues with facilities, infrastructure systems, and community and economic development. These may be basic improvements, but they are giant issues on the funding capacity front, hopefully, set a solid foundation for future growth and development.

Our efforts in community engagement yielded positive outcomes as well for open dialogue and collaboration. The community is rich with its business and non-profit presence. We just started but we witnessed a surge in engagement, investment, and contribution. Our collective efforts as a community are true wealth and have resulted in shared ownership of the community's development agenda. Collaboration with partners played a crucial role in facilitating those major investment benchmarks. The takeaway here is that by fostering an environment of innovation, support, and shared success, we are able to harness the collective talents and resources of the community, contributing to the progressive development of the city. The economic development initiative we implemented also bore fruit. Our targeted campaign and recruitment approach continue to attract prospects, interest, and new development to the city and county, creating more opportunities for stimulating the local economy. Like seeds taking root, these investments will bring renewed vitality to the community, enhancing its vibrancy. In celebrating this benchmark, it is important to acknowledge the hard work and dedication of our employees and volunteers. Their commitment and tireless efforts are instrumental in driving our initiative forward. Whether it being a supportive team, organizing community events, funding, or providing essential services, their contributions are invaluable. Like gears, we work together to ensure the smooth functioning and progress of our beloved city.

It is also important to express gratitude to the broader Osky team. Their support and active participation are vital in making progress possible. They embraced change, shared their ideas, and invested their time and resources in building a better future. Their collective commitment enriched our journey and strengthened our sense of belonging. Those couple of years have laid a foundation, but we have a long way to go and much more to be accomplished. The challenges that lie ahead may be different, but with the same spirit of collaboration, resilience, and determination, I am confident that we will continue to make progress and achieve even greater heights.

Parting Thought

Leadership is not static but a continuous evolution because we, as people, continue to evolve. It's not about grand gestures but about the collective impact of humble steps and shifts in perspectives. As we step forward and up, let's remember the words of the great Winston Churchill: "Success is not final, failure is not fatal. It is the courage to continue that counts." So, whether you're leading a team, a city, or just trying to herd cats in a meeting, keep in mind that awareness, growth, and resilience are your allies. And remember, leading is not a sprint; it's a dance marathon. So, lace up your leadership shoes, embrace the rhythm of growth and waltz into excellence.

As we step out of these pages and back into the hustle and bustle of daily lives, let's carry forward the mindset that propels us ever forward. Here's to leading with a growth mindset, courage, kindness, and a touch of humor. Wishing you a leadership journey filled with more triumphs than tribulations.

Onward and upward!

RECOMMENDED BOOKS

The Advantage: Patrick Lencioni

Discovering Job Joy: Patti Seda

Elevate: Robert Glazer

BIBLIOGRAPHY

Acharya, N. (May 2015). Jack Welch -- Be The 'Chief Meaning Officer'. *Forbes*, https://www.forbes.com/sites/nishacharya/2015/05/19/jack-welch-be-the-chief-meaning-officer/?sh=501106183441.

Achebe, C. (n.d.). *Things Fall Apart, in 1958*.

Biden, J. (n.d.).

Company, McKinsey &. (n.d.). *Some employees are destroying value. Others are building it. Do you know the difference?* Retrieved from https://www.mckinsey.com/capabilities/people-and-organizational-performance/our-insights/some-employees-are-destroying-value-others-are-building-it-do-you-know-the-difference

DeSutter, P. A. (1993, Dec 01). *Sun Tzu, Clausewitz, and the Importance of Knowing Yourself and the Enemy.* Retrieved from DTIC: https://apps.dtic.mil/sti/citations/ADA440962

Fainstein, S. C. (n.d.). *Readings in Planning Theory 2nd Edition.*

Glazer, R. (2019). *Elevate: Push Beyond Your Limits and Unlock Success in Yourself and Others.* Simple Truths.

KIZUNA. (2022, 311). Retrieved from Japan Gov, The Government of Japan: https://www.japan.go.jp/kizuna/2022/03/ikigai_japanese_secret_to_a_joyful_life.html

Lencioni, P. (Mar 13, 2012). *The Advantage: Why Organizational Health Trumps Everything Else in Business.*

Pritzker, G. J. (2023, June 12). Retrieved from Twitter Account: https://twitter.com/GovPritzker

Seda, P. (2020). *Discovering Job Joy: Your Guide to Stretching Without Snapping.* Jones Media Publishing.

Shanmugam, K. (2021). 10 Leadership Lessons from Jack Welch.

Suits Season 4, Episode 15

ABOUT THE AUTHOR

Amal Eltahir is currently serving as the City Manager for Oskaloosa. With six years in city management roles and over a decade of executive leadership experience in the private sector, she has led teams and managed diverse businesses with notable efficiency and foresight. Known as a dynamic force, Eltahir drives progress and innovation, fueled by her passion for growth and development.

Her academic credentials include an M.S. in Urban and Regional Planning from the University of Iowa. Eltahir's professional journey in government began with community development, which expanded to encompass critical responsibilities in city budgets and administration..

As an author passionate about organizational development and leadership, she blends practical industry experience with strategic insight, positioning herself as a highly credible and authoritative figure in management. In Oskaloosa, Eltahir remains focused on fostering a thriving community through thoughtful planning and effective management.

www.ingramcontent.com/pod-product-compliance
Lightning Source LLC
Chambersburg PA
CBHW072349090426
42741CB00012B/2982